Robert Sinker

The Psalm of Habakkuk

A Revised Translation With Exegetical and Critical Notes

Robert Sinker

The Psalm of Habakkuk
A Revised Translation With Exegetical and Critical Notes

ISBN/EAN: 9783337020590

Printed in Europe, USA, Canada, Australia, Japan

Cover: Foto ©ninafisch / pixelio.de

More available books at **www.hansebooks.com**

THE PSALM OF HABAKKUK.

THE
PSALM OF HABAKKUK

A REVISED TRANSLATION, WITH EXEGETICAL AND CRITICAL
NOTES ON THE HEBREW AND GREEK TEXTS,

BY

ROBERT SINKER, B.D.

LIBRARIAN OF TRINITY COLLEGE, CAMBRIDGE.

Cambridge:

DEIGHTON, BELL AND CO.
LONDON: GEORGE BELL AND SONS.
1890.

CAMBRIDGE
PRINTED BY JONATHAN PALMER
ALEXANDRA STREET

INTRODUCTION.

A certain amount of definiteness of view as to the date when Habakkuk uttered his prophecy is essential to the right understanding of his utterance. The means for coming to a conclusion are, it is true, scanty: external objective evidence is altogether wanting, but a reasonable clue is given by the prophet himself. It is necessary to refer, however briefly, to this evidence, inasmuch as the views to be taken of the prophet's standpoint, and especially in the poem to which the whole prophecy works up, will hinge largely on the question of the author's date.

The prophecy, taken as a whole, brings before us the threat of the Chaldæan invasion, the horrors that follow in its train, the overweening arrogance of the invader, his utter inability to see that he is in God's hands but the rod of His anger, and his impious glorifying of his own power, the "axe boasting itself against him that heweth with it." Through and beyond this thunder cloud, itself yet future, the prophet, with vision which the divine insight has rendered keen, looks on, patiently and undoubtingly, to the day when the Chaldæan host itself, its work done, falls beneath a mightier foe.

With these two feelings then filling his heart—with the knowledge that on His people God's wrath is to be poured out, that a race mighty and pitiless is to work His will upon them; but with the fullest belief that beyond the storm of trouble, nay, amid it, God's purpose of mercy fully held,—the Prophet breaks out in this marvellous Psalm, in which the twofold thoughts of the preceding chapters are wrought together, two ideas running connected throughout, till, in the jubilant strain at the end, all is forgotten but the full out-pouring of God's love for His people.

Thus the whole prophecy becomes one connected utterance, the two thoughts of the suffering and the deliverance, dwelt on in the first two chapters, being the underlying fabric of the Psalm; and the repressed force of those earlier chapters breaks out in the utterance, at once earnestly expectant and jubilant, of the conclusion.

The perfect cohesion of the whole book forces one to the belief that we must view it as a perfect artistic whole, presumably given forth at one time.

It is doubtless impossible to fix that time with exactness, but we believe the choice to lie between the concluding years of Manasseh's reign and the opening years of that of Josiah. For this conclusion, two remarks of the prophet stand clearly out, and the whole prophecy accords perfectly.

The two remarks are both contained in the same verse (i. 5); the horrors of the invasion were to be within the actual experience of many of the generation which the prophet addressed, and he knows with what incredulity his words will be received. After the crushing defeat of the Egyptian army by the Chaldæans at Carchemish (605 B.C.) incredulity would have been impossible, and herein we find our posterior limit of time. From this we may go back as far as is consistent with the words, "I work a work in your days." It is folly to inquire within what limits of time this phrase is used in the Bible, and so in this servile way deduce our limits here. It is sufficient to note that from the death of Manasseh (640 B.C.) to the first taking of Jerusalem by the Chaldæans (597 B.C.) is 43 years, so that if the prophecy were delivered in the concluding years of this king's life, a considerable portion of those then living would be surviving when the terrible fulfilment actually came.

Further back than to the concluding years of Manasseh's reign it would be impossible to put the prophecy, not only because we should thus fail to satisfy the condition "in your days," but also because the general character of the reign of Manasseh, "who filled Jerusalem with blood from one end to another," is that of fierce persecution of the worship of Jehovah, and of idolatry dominant, while the standpoint of Habakkuk is that of an age of careless indifference and of mere social wrongs. The prophet sees violence and oppression, but no hint is given that a religious cause underlies it. The law is slack and dead; evidently the zeal and the love of the many has waxed cold. In like manner too, the short evil reign of Amon may be passed over as failing to yield the necessary historical characteristics.

Again, how is it possible to assign the utterance of Habakkuk to a date later than the early years of Josiah? We can hardly conceive the words with which the book opens to have been put forth when once Josiah's reformation had been set on foot. Such words as "the law is slacked" could not have been said when that single-hearted king strove to restore the service of God.

That Habakkuk prophesied early in the reign of Jehoiakim, would be to make the incredulity of the prophet's hearers absurd. When the army of so mighty a kingdom as Egypt had been shattered at Carchemish by the mighty young Titan of Chaldæa, it could not be doubted that the conqueror would in due time move westwards; and before that fierce onset how should Israel stand? Yet if the writing is to be placed, as some would have us place it, even as late as the time of the first appearance of Nebuchadnezzar's armies in Palestine (600 B.C.), the reference to the incredulity is either meaningless, or is put in by the prophet merely to antedate his utterance.

That a writer could indulge in an attempt of this kind and then close the didactic part of his utterance with the solemn words, "The LORD is in His holy temple, let all the earth keep silence before Him," would be a piece of profane audacity which seems incredible—incredible even if we have here but a poet paying a decent recognition to the current religious feeling of his time. Yet on any view of a deeper purpose, of an utterance beyond that of poet, of a thing which comes from no $ἰδία\ ἐπίλυσις$, how impossible any such theory!

It must be remembered, however, that this is really not so much a question between inspiration and not-inspiration, as between honesty of purpose and conscious dishonesty. The theory of the late date of Habakkuk would make of his wondrous prophecy but a cunningly devised scheme, tricked out by poetic fancy. The prophet stands on his watch-tower, not for a revelation sent from heaven, or even for the self-conjured ideas of his own fancy as to what the future may bring; he is simply playing with what he knows.

We repeat then, the concluding years of the reign of Manasseh, or the opening years of that of Josiah, satisfy the two crucial conditions of i. 5, and give us a state of things fully in accordance with what seems to be the standpoint of the prophet.

Like Bunyan's pilgrims, who could see the streets of the Golden City before their feet had come to the edge of the Dark River, so Habakkuk realises the certainty and the glory of God's deliverance while the doom itself is still distant. His thoughts, which seem full of a suppressed force in the earlier part of the prophecy, break forth in free expression in the Psalm, an expression of unwavering faith and trust that God will, as of old, bring His people through the storm. The prophet sees in faith "the end of the Lord"; the deliverance shall certainly come in the appointed time.

With this certainty of the coming mercy, it is natural to blend the thought of the like mercies of the past; "As were Thy dealings of old, so now wilt Thou deal with Thy people." It is in the light of this twofold truth, I am convinced, that much of this Psalm is to be understood. Otherwise, the constantly fluctuating tenses, combined with the most evident allusions to the earlier history, leave us in an unmeaning chaos. That, in vv. 3—15, the continual shifting to and fro of the tenses is to be treated as mere poetic caprice, is both to play fast and loose with all laws of language, and further, rob the poem of much of its significance. If, on the other hand, these tenses are to be distinguished, then we believe that here, as in the most parallel instance of the Sixty-eighth Psalm, the inspired writer's mind dwells, now on his certain assurance of God's future mercy, now on past manifestations of it; not indeed that the proof for the future does but rest on the evidence of the past, but that no

Introduction.

believer can lose sight of the past and its call for thanksgiving in his trust for the future.

In the rendering of the Psalm which is now subjoined, an attempt is made to represent this idea. It may be well to premise however, once for all, that with regard to the exact translation in English of *vv.* 3—15 a legitimate difference of view may well exist, "God will come," "May God come."[1] And yet the two are one. The faith which waits unflinchingly will tell of the coming deliverance for as certain a fact as the past. Yet even the faith which knows—knows as a certain truth— will say, "So grant it, Lord."

[1] We might also, with much fitness, translate "cometh," remembering that "cometh" would not be a present but a future, or rather a future and something more, as *e.g.* ἔρχομαι in Joh. xiv. 18.

CHAPTER I.

THE PSALM OF HABAKKUK.

1 A Prayer of Habakkuk the Prophet, upon Shigionoth.

2 O LORD, I have heard Thy message,[1]
  I have trembled, O LORD, at Thy work ;
  In the midst of years revive it,
  In the midst of years make it known,
  In wrath mayest Thou remember mercy.

3 God will come[2] from Teman,
  And the Holy One from Mount Paran (Selah),
  He, Whose glory *of old* covered the heavens,
  And with Whose[3] praise the earth was filled.

4 And *His* brightness shall be as the light,
  Rays *come forth* from His hand ;
  And there *is* the covert of His might.

5 Pestilence will go before Him,
  And lightnings go forth at His feet,

6 Who *of old* stood and shook[4] the earth,
  Who beheld and drove asunder the nations,
  And the eternal mountains were scattered,
  The everlasting hills were bowed—
  His ways *are* everlasting.

7 Under affliction did I behold the tents of Cushan,
  The curtains of the land of Midian were shaken.

8 Was it with rivers that the LORD was angry?
  Was Thy wrath against the rivers?
  Was Thy fury against the sea,
  That Thou dost ride upon Thy horses,
  Thy chariots of salvation?

---

[1] *Lit.* Thy report, i.e. the news of what Thou wilt do.

[2] *Or,* cometh.

[3] *Or,* Whose praise filled the earth.

[4] *Or,* measured.

The Psalm of Habakkuk.

9 Thy bow is⁵ made quite bare,
   Sworn are the punishments of the⁶ solemn decree (Selah):
   With rivers wilt Thou cleave the earth.
10 The mountains saw Thee, they trembled,
   A storm of waters passed by,
   The deep gave forth his voice,
   And lifted up his hands on high.⁷
11 Sun *and* moon stood still in *their* abode,
   At the light of Thy fast-falling arrows,
   At the brightness of the gleam of Thy spear.
12 In indignation wilt Thou march through the earth,
   In anger wilt Thou tread down the nations,
13 As when Thou wentest forth for the salvation of Thy people,
   For the salvation⁸ of Thine anointed,
   And didst dash the head from the house of the wicked,
   Laying bare the foundation even to the neck (Selah),
14 When Thou didst pierce with his own staves the head of his chieftains,⁹
   Who come as a whirlwind to scatter me,
   Whose exulting is as though to devour the poor in their lair,
15 When Thou didst tread on the sea with Thy horses,
   The foaming mass of mighty waters.

16 I heard, and my belly trembled,
   At *the* voice my lips quivered,
   Rottenness cometh into my bones and I tremble where I stand,
   I, who will wait peacefully for the day of trouble,
   For the coming up against *the* people of him who shall assail it.
17 For though the fig tree shall not blossom,
   Nor shall there be fruit in the vines,
   Though the labour of the olive shall have failed,
   And the fields shall have yielded no food,
   Though the flock shall have been cut off from the fold,
   And there be no cattle in the stalls,
18 Yet will I exult in the LORD,
   I will be glad in the God of my salvation.

⁵ See note, p. 5.
⁶ *Or*, of *Thy Word*.
⁷ *Or*, The height lifted up...
⁸ *Or*, salvation with...
⁹ *Or*, hordes.

19 Jehovah, the Lord, is my strength,
And He hath made my feet like hinds' feet,
And on my high places will He make me to walk.

To the Chief Musician, on my stringed instruments.

The Psalm may be roughly analysed as follows:

v. 1. The heading with the title of the poem, "a Prayer," and the manner of its music.

v. 2 is the prelude to the main body of the poem, *vv.* 3—15, the reverent supplication of the Prophet, awestruck even amid the faith which looks on to the end.

vv. 3—7. The looked for manifestation of God's presence and glory as of old.

vv. 8—12, detailed illustrations of the effect of God's presence on nature, rivers, sea, mountains, sun, and moon.

Yet (*vv.* 13—15) the terrors of this appearing are not for God's people, but for the enemy.

vv. 16—19 form a conclusion, as though the reflections of the Psalmist to himself, at the consideration of such unspeakable marvels; awe, yet the awe of exceeding joy. Amid the desolation of nature he looks on to the final deliverance, and sees in the Lord his strength.

Lastly, a musical direction is subjoined.

---

v. 1. תְּפִלָּה. The Psalm is not indeed precatory in *form*, for *v.* 2 is the only part which can directly and formally be called a prayer. Still the underlying thought is distinctly precatory throughout. Whether it be the dwelling on God's wonders in the past, the anticipations of like mercies in the future, the

The Psalm of Habakkuk.

awful circumstances attending the manifestations of His Power— in all alike one thought is present, the prayer that in due time God will grant the deliverance of His people.[1] The same remark, *mutatis mutandis*, may in greater or less degree be applied to the case of those Psalms (xvii., lxxxvi., xc., cii.) which are styled "Prayer" in the heading; and with these may be compared the remark at the end of the Second Book of Psalms, "The prayers of David the son of Jesse are ended." It must be noticed, too, that it is not simply "a Prayer of Habakkuk," but of "Habakkuk *the Prophet*"; the Prayer is more than the earnest struggling of a soul after the Divine Light, it is definitely the prayer as shaped for him by the guidance of the Holy Spirit.

עַל שִׁגְיוֹנוֹת. — This expression has been understood by some to refer to sins ignorantly committed. Thus the verse is rendered in the Targum, "The prayer which Habakkuk the Prophet prayed when it was revealed to him concerning the length of time which He has given to the wicked, that if they will turn to the law with a perfect heart it shall be forgiven them, and all their trespasses which they have committed in His sight shall be like a sin unwittingly committed." Or again, it has been explained (*e.g.* Jerome, *in loc.*; Rashi, *in loc.*) of the sins of which the prophet was unwittingly guilty in his addresses to God (as in i. 2—4, 13, 14).

Still, in spite of such authorities, such a view seems untenable when it is considered that the Psalm contains no reference to sins of ignorance. Considering, too, the frequent use of the preposition עַל in the headings of the Psalms,[2] and the fact that in that to Psalm vii. the word שִׁגָּיוֹן itself occurs, where such a rendering is altogether impossible, we can hardly doubt

---

[1] The assertion that תְּפִלָּה here is simply, in a general sense, a *hymn* (Ges.) requires proof. To attempt to justify it by the use of the verb in 1 Sam. ii. 1 is to ignore the fact that, praise though it is, prayer is the underlying basis of both Hannah's song and its close counterpart, the *Magnificat*.

[2] It is true that עַל most often introduces the name of the standard melody, but sometimes it indicates simply the musical mode generally, *e.g.* on Alamoth.

that the phrase has reference to the nature of the musical accompaniment to the poem.

From the meaning of the root we might render the phrase "a wild, wandering strain," the reference being to the constant varying of the melody, as it adapted itself to the thoughts of the terrors of God's judgements wrought upon His enemies, of the marvels done in the past, of the deliverances to be wrought for His people.[1]

The ancient versions seem all to have taken the earlier view, except the LXX., which renders the phrase by μετὰ ᾠδῆς. This is loose enough, but would seem to be decisive as to their opinion; unless indeed we believe that the LXX. confused the word with הִגָּיוֹן, which is rendered ᾠδή in Pss. ix. 17; xcii. 4.[2]

v. 2. In every sense this verse is a prelude to the Psalm which follows. Not again till *v.* 16, after the close of the wondrous Theophany, is the personality of the writer brought before us. He has heard the Divine Message, he trembles at the thought of what God is about to work, even though that work will ultimately result in the deliverance of God's people. Yet there is a momentary pause, as when Moses stands barefoot and in silence before the Burning Bush on Horeb. In the hush we seem to hear the pulsations of the prophet's heart, in which trembling awe at the reception of God's message and passionate earnestness of appeal are blended. Then suddenly he bursts forth into the glorious utterance, at once prophecy and prayer, which bridges over the chasm of trouble and sees the deliverance effected.

— שִׁמְעֲךָ. "Thy message." The word שֵׁמַע is literally "a hearing," whether the faculty of hearing or the thing heard. Thus it will be tidings or news about a person or thing, and so here, the tidings of God's work which He has given to the prophet. We may compare Isa. lxvi. 19, "the far-off isles which

---

[1] It may be noticed that the main thought of Psalm vii. is also that of God's judgements on the wicked and the deliverance of the righteous.

[2] Their rendering of *Shiggaion* in the heading of Ps. vii. is ὕμνος.

had not heard my fame (*or*, the news of me)." Thus the meaning is much the same as "message."[1] *Cf.* Hos. vii. 12.

The message in question is clearly the whole of the preceding part of the prophet's utterance, not merely i. 5—10. To say that the message of ch. ii. would arouse no fear in the mind of the prophet is surely to take a very false view of the position of the God-fearing soul in the direct presence, nay, behind the veil as it were, of the Divine working. The most steadfast servant of Jehovah must have felt his heart stand still, in the very fulness of his joy and thankfulness, when he saw the waters of the Red Sea "return to their strength" and the Egyptians dead upon the sea shore. Keble takes a truer view of the situation when he says, "It was a *fearful* joy to trace the Heathen's toil." What though there was but chastening for Israel, and though God's destroying wrath was for the enemy, yet to be admitted to see the working of God in anger, must surely be awful for all.

— ... יָרֵאתִי. I am aware that the translation given of this clause is not that ordinarily taken, and I fully allow that it is not that grouping of the words sanctioned by the Masoretic accents. Still, I venture to think that the present translation is defensible.

For (1), if we accept the rendering, "I trembled, O Lord, at Thy work," we make the whole of *vv.* 2—6 reducible to ternary *stichi*, as may be seen from the annexed table:

v. 2. 3 3 3 3.
v. 3. 3 3 3 3.
v. 4. 3 3 3.
v. 5. 3 3.
v. 6. 3 3 3 3.

In *v.* 7 the rhythm changes, but that of the bulk of the rest of the Psalm is also in ternary *stichi*. In the ordinary translation the above regularity is of course not attained.

---

[1] It is true that שֶׁמַע is rather news *about* a person than a message sent *by* a person, but the conditions of the case in Hab. iii. 2 make these two things one.

Again (2), if we inquire concerning the grammatical usage of the verb ירא in the Bible, we find that there are 111 cases in which it is used absolutely, as against 155 cases where it has an objective, whether introduced by אֵת, מִן, or the like. At any rate, therefore, there is no violence done to the grammar in construing as I have done.

It must first be asked, however, what is the פֹּעַל of God here? Clearly not that of i. 5, for that is simply the chastisement of Israel, which the prophet could not conceivably pray for.[1] We cannot doubt that it is the exact correlative to the שָׁמַע of the preceding clause. The prophet has heard the message; he trembles at the work that message foreshadows.

That work we have already defined as chastisement wrought upon Israel for its sins at the hands of an enemy whose own doom is utter destruction. But clearly if this be so, the essence of the matter is the former part of the thought. To the Israelite, knowing that he had deserved God's discipline, that discipline, stern but loving, just yet overflowing with mercy, was the main thought. That the rod of God's anger, its purpose done, should be snapped in twain, mattered not.[2]

— ... בְּקֶרֶב. This phrase, it must be allowed, is somewhat obscure. The meaning must, however, hinge mainly on the verb. Gesenius (*Thes.* p. 468 a) gives for the Piel of חיה three meanings (1) *vivere jussit, vivificavit;* (2) *vivum servavit;* (3) *in vitam revocavit.* We might reduce these three to two, viz. (*a*) to call into existence a thing not previously existent, or, if once existent, dead; and (*b*) to maintain in life a thing already living. I must say that I do not think this former

---

[1] To suppose that the פֹּעַל is Israel itself, because (Isa. lx. 21) Israel is called the "work" (מַעֲשֵׂה) of God's hands is out of the question; for not only should we require some qualifying word instead of this bare absolute use, but also because while the verb חַיֵּיהוּ might thus have a reasonable meaning, תּוֹדִיעַ (the same object being of course presupposed) would not. It should be noted, however, that this view is that taken by Aben Ezra and Kimchi.

[2] A very parallel passage, which has some striking coincidences with the present, is Ps. lxxvii. 13, where the פֹּעַל of God is clearly the whole course of God's dealings with His people.

meaning at all established. It must be remembered that the Piel of חיה is common in the Bible, occurring as it does no less than 57 times, and in the bulk of these the meaning is obvious enough. No better illustration could be taken than Abraham's remark to Sarah (Gen. xii. 12), "They will kill me, but they will save thee alive (יְחַיּוּ)."

It is worth while taking in order Gesenius's instances of the first of his three meanings: (1) Job xxxiii. 4. Here Ges. renders the second clause, "Spiritus Omnipotentis vitam mihi dedit." But this is surely utterly to disregard the change of tense from past to future: "The Spirit of God made me" (the actual creation), "and the breath of the Almighty keepeth me in life." One is reminded of the change from ἐκτίσθη to ἔκτισται in Col. i. 15. The next instance (Gen. xix. 33, 34) is perhaps more doubtful, yet even here it would be quite possible to explain the phrase as meaning "to keep alive the family line." Hos. xiv. 8 is also doubtful, but it seems hard to believe that יְחַיּוּ דָגָן can mean "they shall grow crops of corn." Such a passage, however, as Eccl. vii. 12 ought to be clear enough, "Wisdom preserveth alive" (not "calleth to life") "those that possess it." So, too, Job xxxvi. 6, "[God] preserveth not in life" (not "calleth to life") "a wicked man."

We need not go through the passages given under Gesenius's third head, but they are as a rule utterly beside the mark. Thus it is a begging of the question to make 1 Sam. ii. 6 mean a "recalling to life"; surely the clause is tantamount to the statement that God gives (as and when He will) life and death likewise. The call into life therefore is only part of the gift; we have to thank God for "our creation *and* preservation." See also Deut. xxxii. 39, or again Ps. xxx. 4, "Thou hast kept me alive, so that I go not down into the pit" (*Kri*, but the *Cthiv* is to all intents and purposes much the same). We need not multiply instances, and the fact remains that in the great majority of 57 instances there can be no possible doubt as to the meaning; and even of the remainder it may reasonably be questioned whether any single one is an undoubted exception.

If, then, this view be accepted, Habakkuk's prayer is that

God will *keep* alive His work; that work, I have argued, is His discipline of Israel. Discipline is not punishment, though it may involve it. Coming from God to His people, there underlies the punishment the tenderest love.

The remainder of the clause is less obvious. God is asked to keep alive and to make known His work of loving discipline בְּקֶרֶב שָׁנִים, a phrase not occurring elsewhere. It has indeed by some been understood of the coming of Christ "in the midst of years," with the ages of the two dispensations before it and after it. The view in this form, however, is clearly untenable. The Psalm is indeed Messianic in its deeper sense, but not in its direct and primary one. Moreover, קֶרֶב could by no means be used of the middle point of a thing; it is, if I may so speak, τὸ ἔσω rather than τὸ μέσον.

As regards the meaning of the phrase, Gesenius may be right in his rendering "intra (aliquos, paucos) annos," there being, as I have said, no parallel instance; but I do not think he is. The general sense resulting from his view would be "help us speedily." But the "work" of God in this passage is not *directly* help, but severe though loving chastening. The chastening is but for a time, and then God's wrath is to be poured on the Chaldæans. Thus, on the view of Gesenius, the prayer would come to mean, Let us get our punishment over quickly and have done with it. But further, if I have been successful in showing that חַיֵּיהוּ does not mean "bring to life," but "keep alive," the meaning of *speedily* must obviously fall to the ground.

If it then be asked what translation of בְּקֶרֶב שָׁנִים is possible in conjunction with the meaning "keep alive," it seems to me that, having regard to the difference between קֶרֶב and תָּוֶךְ, we might render "in the course of years," "as years roll on." In other words, Be the time of Thy working long or short, yet amid the on-rolling years ever keep alive Thy mercy (mercy, be it remembered, was the essence of the chastening), amid the wrath which we have deserved, mayest Thou evermore remember mercy.

The Psalm of Habakkuk. 15

Rashi, who understands by God's "work" here His ancient work when He took vengeance for Israel on their enemies, explains the phrase now before us by "in the midst of the years of calamity in which we are now abiding." Kimchi, while understanding the "work" as meaning the righteous, explains the phrase as meaning "in the midst of these long years through which they shall be in captivity."

v. 3. The question of the tenses (כִּסָּה, יָבוֹא) first calls for remark. If it be asked whether we are to translate the former "[God] will come," or "May [God] come," we can but repeat that we believe both thoughts are wrought up together; we have at once the prayer of the faith which knows, and the declaration of the knowledge which God grants in vision. To narrow the meaning to one of these conjoined thoughts would be, I am convinced, to sacrifice an important element of the truth.[1]

In יָבוֹא the prophet looks onward, has regard to God's future mercies, as in כִּסָּה he looks back to the days when God wrought wonderfully for His people. The ideas are very elliptically expressed, and various turns in English will be equally true for filling up the gap. We may say, "God will come .... Whose glory of old covered ....," or "God will come .... as of old when His glory covered ....," or in other ways.

The *Selah* of this verse may claim a passing remark. It being assumed that the word carries with it the idea of an

---

[1] Prof. Driver cites *vv.* 3, 7, of this chapter as furnishing cases of the imperfect [future] "to represent an event while nascent (γιγνόμενον), and so, by seizing upon it while in movement rather than while at rest, to picture it with peculiar vividness to the mental eye," this holding good specially "in the language of poetry or prophecy" (*Hebrew Tenses*, § 26, 27 *a*; *cf.* also § 35). I will refer to the case of *v.* 7 subsequently. As regards *v.* 3, I cannot but say that the above seems to me (while of course true for many passages) to be a totally untenable view as regards the tenses in this verse. It treats יָבוֹא and כִּסָּה (and of course we must add the like cases in *vv.* 5, 6, and elsewhere) as in *essence* the same, only differing in the way in which the action is viewed. Thus throughout the whole passage, *vv.* 3—15, whether the tense be past or future ["imperfect"], we are on this theory to view them alike as simply descriptive.

interlude, and so of a brief pause as regards the singing, there will often naturally be implied the presence of a certain transition of thought, and thus there might reasonably be a change of melody. In the present passage the transition of thought enters abruptly, and, so to speak, in the very heart of the rhythm. With the line of thought so absolutely shifted round, we can well understand that the music in the two clauses would be totally different. We may find somewhat parallel cases below, v. 10, and in Ps. lv. 20.

With regard to the reference to Teman and Paran, of which I have spoken further in the next chapter, it is clear that we must view them in connection with the parallel passages, Deut. xxxiii. 2, Judges v. 4, 5, Ps. lxviii. 8, 9. In the first of these, we find Sinai, Seir, and Mount Paran mentioned together, the last-named being either equivalent to the great desert of Paran, or, with greater likelihood, an individual mountain in the Sinaitic peninsula. In the Song of Deborah we have Seir, Edom, and Sinai named; and in a passage of the Sixty-eighth Psalm, evidently built on a reminiscence of the preceding, Sinai alone is named.

Now, it is clear that in poetry of this kind it would be quite possible to aim at a too excessive geographical exactness. Sinai and Seir are by no means near together, nor are Teman and Mount Paran. Moreover, the thread of association in all four passages is so unmistakeable that in any interpretation we are bound to take cognizance of all.

The line of thought seems to be of this sort. The prophet calls to mind the long desert march in the days of old, when God, like a mighty conqueror, moved at the head of His people, displaying wondrous manifestations of His power. His thoughts turn to the wild and mysterious south land with which the associations of the past were so completely bound up, the deliverances amidst the perils of the wilderness, and the solemn giving forth of the Law on Sinai. Then comes the prayer, the hope, the belief, that He, once Victor over all foes for His people, will again be their Champion amid greater dangers and against mightier foes.

The Psalm of Habakkuk. 17

The translation of תֵּימָן by "south" (as by the Vulgate "ab Austro") is rather a dilution of this than a contradiction. The survey of the paths trodden by the Israelites of old, following where the Divine Leader pointed the way, guided the prophet's thoughts.

v. 4. Here the prophet dwells on the Manifestations of God's presence; gleaming brightness attends Him, rays flash from His hand, and amid this splendour, this φῶς ἀπρόσιτον, the Deity "shrouded in eternal brilliance," dwells alone.

The dual קַרְנַיִם is to be accounted for by the original idea of the metaphor. From the primary meaning of "horn" readily springs that of a "ray of light" (whence the denominative verb קָרַן in Exod. xxxiv. 29, 30). Thus the idea of duality naturally passes from the primary to the derived meaning; and so too is clearly obtained the notion of the sun as the "hind of the morning."

The change from שָׁם to שָׂם, as made by the LXX. and Peshito, seems quite uncalled for. Not only is the existing Hebrew supported by two independent versions, the Targum and Vulgate, but שָׂם seems a tame and prosaic alteration, arising from the failure to perceive the force, poetic rather than grammatical, of שָׁם, "amid the splendour."

v. 5. The tenses in this verse make it clear that the prophet looks onward. It is the future manifestation of God's glory that attracts his thoughts; but here again the future is pictured according to the experience of the known past, *v.* 6 serving as a historic basis on which the prophetic expectation of the preceding verse rests. The two verses bear to each other the same relation as do the two hemistichs of *v.* 3. "Pestilence will go before Him, and the lightnings go forth at His feet" to work God's wrath on the enemy. How impossible in such a context to avoid recurring in thought to the manifestations of Divine wrath on God's enemies of old; the dread vengeance yet to come finds sufficient parallels in the past.

Of the "pestilence" one example had been given not so long before the prophet's own times, in the destruction of the

2

host of Sennacherib; or we might take such a case as the dread punishment inflicted in older times on the men of Beth-Shemesh. It forms a natural parallel to רֶשֶׁף, the lightning; unless indeed, though this seems hardly necessary, we translate the latter by "burning disease."[1]

v. 6. וַיְמֹדֶד. That this word should probably be translated "shook" rather than "measured," see a note in the following chapter.

— וַיַּתֵּר. It seems at any rate most probable, though it may not be certain, that we have to deal with two distinct roots נתר in the Bible, starting respectively from the primary notions of (1) *leaping*, (2) *dropping, or flowing off*.

Thus of (1) we have the Kal in Job xxxvii. 1, of the heart palpitating; the Piel in Lev. xi. 21, of locusts, etc. Thus, if our present passage is to be connected with this root, we get for the Hiphil "to make to leap," *i.e.* to make to tremble.

On the other hand, we have in Chaldee the root נתר in Pehal with the meaning *to drop off*. (*Cf.* the following in *Targ. Jon.*, Isa. xl. 8, of a flower; Isa. lxiv. 6, of a leaf; Joel i. 10, of olive-trees; Nah. i. 4, of cedars; Jer. xlviii. 37, of hair). Thus in Aphel we have the meaning of *cause to drop off, shake off*, as in Dan. iv. 11 (14 E. V.).

In connection with this latter root we may place those instances of the Hiphil in the Bible where the sense is that of *loosening* or *breaking loose*; as of actual bonds, as in Isa. lviii. 6, or, by an easy transition, of those bound, Pss. cv. 20, cxlvi. 27 (and metaph. Job vi. 9).

If, then, the word now before us is to be referred to this latter sense, we must understand it of *shaking*, and so *scattering hither and thither*; and hence we get the *drove asunder* of the E. V.[2]

---

[1] This is Kimchi's view: חלי הקדחת

[2] For some remarks as to the possible identity of the two roots, see Dr. Chance in his *Appendix* to his edition of Dr. Bernard's Job (vi. 9). He compares the German *springen* and *sprengen*.

The Psalm of Habakkuk.

v. 6. הֲלִיכוֹת עוֹלָם לוֹ. The line of thought here seems to be this. Even the mountains, which, as generation after generation of men came and passed away, seemed to remain unchangingly, as though themselves eternal, even these mighty masses are scattered and brought low before the presence of God. But, while applying such words as עַד and עוֹלָם to created things, the prophet can but think of One who was eternal in another sense than they—"His goings are everlasting."

Ewald takes the words differently, and implies a repetition of שַׁחוּ again in the last clause, "The ancient hills bowed, the ancient paths before him," *i.e.* the paths across the hills used for so many generations of men. He gives, however, no grounds why this should be preferred, and we cannot but feel that it is much less probable than the preceding.

It may be worth while to examine the last clause somewhat, and first we may consider the versions. The LXX. has βουνοὶ αἰώνιοι πορείας αἰωνίας αὐτοῦ, that is to say, the eternal hills are themselves the eternal pathway of God. This view has found supporters in modern times,[1] but it surely suffices to condemn it that it makes the eternity of God and of the hills co-ordinate. The Peshito has "His goings are from eternity." The Targum, it is true, paraphrases הליכות, by "might," putting גבורת עלמא דיליה, but otherwise agrees with the current view. Finally the Vulgate ("ab itineribus æternitatis ejus"), though not absolutely agreeing, does not materially differ from the preceding.

To recur now to Ewald's view, it may further be objected that שחח in Kal never occurs in the Bible with לְ following,[2] and that as applied to *paths*, שחח is a very curious verb to have at all. Lastly, it may well be doubted whether the word הליכות so certainly means the *via trita* which this view requires. It only occurs in five places in the Bible beside the present. Of these, Ps. lxviii. 25 (*bis*) refers in a very special sense to God, Job vi. 19 is used of travelling companies,

---

[1] So *e.g.* Hitzig, "uralte Pfade Gottes."
[2] Once indeed with לִפְנֵי.

Prov. xxxi. 27 has regard to the management of a household, and Nah. ii. 6 to the act of going ("as they go"). Considering the close resemblance in many ways between the two poems, Ps. lxviii. 25 is clearly a very parallel instance to the present, and here it may be presumed that the "ways" are God's eternal ways of working. See also Ps. lxxvii. 14.

v. 7. Here, in the ראיתי, the prophet puts himself back amid the scenes of the past, and so, speaking from the standpoint of the past, he dwells on the disasters which befell Israel's foes of old.

The meaning of the Hebrew itself calls for no special remark: "I saw the tents of Cushan beneath affliction," *i.e.* bowed down under calamity; under the outpouring of God's wrath Cushan had been overwhelmed. אָוֶן is used here in much the same sense as עָמָל, with which it is parallel in Hab. i. 3, Isa. lix. 4. See also Ps. lv. 4.

The versions vary considerably. The Peshito, while representing the passage verbally, appears to have viewed אָוֶן as a proper name. The Targum, though amplifying the passage, has evidently caught the sense, "When the house of Israel worshipped idols, I delivered them into the hand of the wicked Cushan; but when they returned to observe the Law, 1 wrought for them miracles and mighty deeds, and delivered them from the hand of the Midianites by the hand of Gideon, the son of Joash." That is to say, the reference is understood of the catastrophe befalling the ancient foes of the nation.

The LXX. has taken shelter in literalness (ἀντὶ κόπων εἶδον), but it seems very doubtful what view, if any, these words conveyed to the translators. The ideas which the authors of the versions of the LXX. have tried to convey will be spoken of in the following chapter. The Vulgate, following on the lines of the LXX., has "Pro iniquitate vidi ....." What Jerome himself understood by this may be gathered from his commentary (*in loc.*), and clearly cannot be taken seriously.[1]

---

[1] " Æthiopes tetri .... dæmones intelliguntur, quorum fit tabernaculum quicunque in hoc sæculo propter honores et divitias laborarit; quod significanter sub uno verbo iniquitatis ostenditur ...."

The Psalm of Habakkuk. 21

The reference to the name Cushan is by no means clear. The Targum, as is clearly shown by the added epithet, identifies it with Cushan Rishathaim, and this is the view of the great Rabbinic commentators, Rashi,[1] Aben Ezra, and Kimchi. Of the other versions, the Peshito reproduces the Hebrew verbally, and the LXX. and Vulgate treat כושן as equivalent to כוש, or Æthiopia.

The objection urged against the traditional Palestinian view is the lack of chronological arrangement in thus putting the deliverances wrought by Othniel and Gideon before such earlier incidents as the passage of the Red Sea and of the Jordan (v. 8). Also, it is said, this view involves a greater amount of detail than could be looked for in such a context. The second objection looks too much like a begging of the question, but the first may be allowed to have some weight. Still, when it is remembered how great an impression the miraculous deliverance wrought against Midian through Gideon made on the Israelite mind (see Isa. ix. 4, x. 26, Ps. lxxxiii. 10), it seems hard, in spite of the chronology, not to accept this as the meaning of the second clause. But in that case the objection to Cushan Rishathaim falls to the ground; and it obviously is quite possible that the deliverance from this oppressor may have been attended with mightier signs of intervention than we might be led to infer from the shortness of the account in the Book of Judges.

Yet, on the other hand, the identification of Cushan with Cush has difficulties of its own. The former word occurs nowhere else but here, so that the *actual* evidence is narrowed to that of the LXX. and Vulgate, which need not count for much. Such an argument as Hitzig's, that Cushan may well be the same as Cush, on the analogy of Lotan (one of the "dukes" of Edom, in Gen. xxxvi. 36) for Lot, is to confound illustration and demonstration; and those who hold this view appear to forget that while the etymology of Lot and Lotan is doubtless

---

[1] Rashi does not *expressly* name Cushan Rishathaim, but accepts the explanation given in the Targum.

the same, it by no means follows thence that the names are interchangeable.[1]

It might further be urged, that by accepting this view we not only give a good deal of vagueness to the passage, but also a certain bathos if, after reading of the awful manifestations of v. 6, we get in v. 7 merely a statement that two nations were much alarmed thereby; whereas on the other view there is reference in v. 7 to directly miraculous intervention.

Ewald, who quite rejects the Cush theory, suggests that כּוּשָׁן is probably the same as יָקְשָׁן (Gen. xxv. 2, 3), viewed as a tribe or a nation cognate with Midian. This is, however, the merest guess; and one does not see by what legitimate modification of spelling the two forms can be treated as equivalent.[2]

A remark may perhaps be added as to the tenses in this verse. I can have no doubt that the future יִרְגְּזוּן is to be seen as under the influence of the past רָאִיתִי, as below in v. 10 (Driver, *Hebrew Tenses*, § 27, γ). In the present passage, however, as I have mentioned above under v. 3, Prof. Driver explains the tense as "representing the event while nascent" (§ 26, 27, *a*). I cannot see why he should not have included it in his list of examples where an "imperfect" [future] follows immediately after a perfect, indicating "the rapid or instantaneous manner in which the second action is conceived as following the first" (*ib.* § 27, γ), amid which he includes Hab. iii. 10.

It is true that יִרְגְּזוּן does not follow *immediately* upon the foregoing past tense, as in the instance of v. 10, but this remark holds equally for several of Prof. Driver's own examples (Exod. xv. 12, 14; Pss. xlvi. 6, lxix. 33, lxxiv. 14, lxxvii. 17).

v. 8. With this verse a fresh strophe of the poem begins, and with examples drawn from the period of the Exodus and of

---

[1] Maurer's suggestion that Cush is altered into Cushan, so as to give a termination harmonising with that of Midian, has perhaps some plausibility, but lacks evidence.

[2] Ewald remarks that the conclusion of strophe 2 (*vv.* 6, 7) "has not been preserved in its full extent." This is indeed to play the part of "I am Sir Oracle"; there is not one vestige of evidence for this reckless statement.

the occupation of Canaan, God is pictured as a warrior once more about to take the field against His foes. The change of tense in the verse has clearly to be borne in mind, as introducing a transition of thought like those we have previously considered.

On the view we have already advocated, the general sense of the verse would be, "When God's wonders were shown on the Red Sea and the Jordan, was the Sea or the River the subject of God's wrath? Surely that power manifested on Sea and on River was the outcome of God's wrath on Egyptian and on Canaanite. So, too, again is it now. Is it against Sea or River that Thou art wroth, that Thou ridest as a warrior to the fight and for deliverance of Thy people? No, for the Chaldæan is the foe."

I cannot but believe, in spite of some objections, that in the first clause of the verse יהוה is the nominative to חרה, the change from the third person of the first clause to the second person in the second clause being very characteristic of Hebrew. We thus get the translation, "Was it with rivers that the Lord was angry? or against the rivers Thy wrath? or against the sea Thy fury?"

On the other view, the יהוה is a vocative, the nominative to חרה being the אפך of the following clause. It is sometimes said that the ancient versions, save the Peshito, do treat יהוה as a vocative. But it must be remembered that we have only got three other independent versions; that the Targum is, as might have been expected, too paraphrastic to give any clue; and that the LXX., though reading a vocative, is in no sense a supporter of the second rendering, inasmuch as it treats each of the two ternary *stichi* at the beginning of the verse as a complete sentence, and thus agrees virtually, though not formally, with the former of the two renderings. Lastly, the Vulgate is but the echo of the LXX.

A more serious matter is the fact that there is no parallel instance to the construction of חרה used in direct agreement with a person. Still there seems a much greater improbability in having two consecutive clauses, of which the first contains the

v. 9. The metaphor of the Divine Warrior marching against His foes is continued in this verse (see also *vv.* 11 *b*, 12, etc.). The bow is bared, drawn forth from its case, so as to be ready for action; the noun עֶרְיָה giving the same kind of emphasis that the presence of an infinitive absolute would have done. It is made quite bare, it is no mere sign or threat of judgement which may yet be averted, the day of vengeance is indeed come.

The clause which follows is one of exceeding difficulty, and the views put forth concerning it differ very widely. I propose simply to refer to various views, only so far as may be necessary to explain or defend the view which seems to me the most probable.

The first word שְׁבֻעוֹת has been variously taken as (1) the plural of שְׁבוּעָה an oath; (2) the plural of שָׁבוּעַ; or (3) the 2nd participle Kal (fem. pl.) of שׂבע.

Again מַטּוֹת may have the meaning of (1) a staff or rod, or (2) a tribe. Lastly, אֹמֶר is a purely poetical word, which as a rule carries with it the idea of a solemn promise, or utterance of solemn import.[1]

As regards שְׁבֻעוֹת, I cannot but think that the third meaning is to be preferred for several reasons. For (1) in this way alone is the second *stichus* of the verse a co-ordinate clause with the preceding, and so is more in harmony with the general style of the poem. Again, if with the E. V. and the Jewish authorities generally we take the meaning of "oaths," the word אֹמֶר is left awkwardly stranded, in a way which seems very improbable. It is true that the second view avoids this, but

---

[1] Thus we find it used for the solemn promise of God (Pss. lxviii. 12, lxxvii. 9), and for the "wondrous tale" which day tells to day and night to night of the Creator's power (Ps. xix. 3, 4). In the one remaining place where we find it in the Old Testament, Job xxii. 28, it is used more generally, like דָּבָר.

only to introduce fresh difficulties of its own. This is the view adopted by Ewald, "Siebenfache Geschosse des Krieges."

Against this, however, a rather serious objection may be urged; it is obtained, as we have seen, by treating the word under consideration as the plural of שָׁבוּעַ, so that the literal translation would thus be "Heptads of darts . . . . ." But although this last named word occurs twenty times in the Bible, it is always used to indicate a week, a heptad of *days*, except when (Daniel ix. 24 sqq.) it is used for a heptad of *years*. It therefore entirely begs the question to assume that it may be used here for bundles of seven darts.

As regards מַטּוֹת, the Jewish interpreters (*e.g.* Targum, Rashi, Kimchi) have as a rule taken it as meaning the tribes of Israel. Aben Ezra, as will be mentioned below, takes it differently. The LXX., which goes very far afield, will be discussed in the following chapter; the Vulgate has "juramenta tribubus," but the Peshito has treated שְׁבוּעוֹת as though from שֶׁבַע, though making מַטּוֹת to be "darts."

This meaning of "rod" or "staff" or "dart" is very common in the Bible, and in various aspects, whether of support or of attack. Thus in Isa. x. 5, xxx. 32, Mic. vi. 10, the rod is that of correction and punishment. Considering the *special* nature of the imagery here, the metaphor of the warrior with his bow, and also the use of the word below in *v.* 14, I should be disposed to think it possible that the metaphor may be strictly pressed, and that the מַטֶּה is not so much a rod to strike, as a javelin or dart to hurl.

It will have been seen that it is not easy to settle what to do with אֹמֶר if שְׁבוּעוֹת be taken in any way except the last named. I would therefore explain the clause, "Promised by oath are the punishments which Thy foes are now to undergo, and which are pledged in Thy word to Thy people," אֹמֶר thus taking the notion of "promise" if seen from the standpoint of Israel, and of "solemn decree" if from that of the foe. I would point out that, to say nothing of objections urged above to the other views, the verse seems on this view to cohere in a way resembling that of other parts of the Psalm, as though it said,

"Thy bow is utterly bared, and Thou wilt indeed execute Thy vengeance, for now as of old Thy threats of punishment upon Thy foes have been put on solemn record."[1]

As regards the grammatical connection of the word אֹמֶר with those before it, I should prefer not to call it, as some do, an "adverbial accusative," or to supply a preposition before it, but to assume that מַטּוֹת is in construction with it. "The rod of the decree" is no more awkward than the "rod of doom" (or, destiny) in Isa. xxx. 32, where the grammar is free from ambiguity, or than the "rod (שֵׁבֶט) of his mouth" in Isa. xi. 4.[2]

The *Selah*, as before (*v.* 3), breaks the strain, not as on the former occasion with a kind of antithesis, but as leading to the outcome of what had gone before, the catastrophe as it were. I render the clause, "With rivers Thou wilt rend the earth," *i.e.* the manifestations of God's power and wrath, the quaking mountains, the beating storm, the tossing waves of the sea, are accompanied by the rending and tearing of the earth, in which torrents burst forth from the chasms. Thus in *vv.* 8, 9*a*, we have, as it were, the storm of wrath in anticipation; from the *Selah* onwards we have the tokens of its outburst.

The clause has been rendered in several different ways, but I venture to think that the above is much to be preferred. I would argue that the verb is in the second person rather than

---

[1] The present view is substantially that of Aben Ezra, though, with what seems absurdity, he understands the "bow" of the rain-bow. He then remarks "The meaning of שׁם has regard to the arrows, ... as though the darts were sworn to establish Thy word."

[2] A commentator, whose remarks are as a rule characterised both by great good sense and sound scholarship, Maurer, has deserted this view which he formerly held (1) as being too artificial, (2) because we should expect a clause conforming to the warlike metaphor of the preceding, and (3) because it would be more reasonable to treat מטה as in *v.* 14. The first point is a purely subjective remark; but as regards the other two, the view I have taken of supposing the general meaning of *rod* here to assume the more special meaning of *dart* seems to meet the case. This "too artificial" view Maurer gives up for "satiatæ sanguine sunt hastæ, epinicium," *i.e.* שְׁבֻעוֹת is to be changed into שְׂבֵעוֹת on the authority of the Peshito, and אֹמֶר to be little more than a sort of interjection.

The Psalm of Habakkuk. 27

the third, because, besides the grammatical reason, to be mentioned presently, we seem to need some *direct* mention of the Deity, whether as subject or object, when beginning the turn of thought which the *Selah* introduces.

Again, as regards the verb, the Piel of בקע occurs twelve times in the Bible, and in every case but one is followed by *the thing actually torn or rent* as a direct object, *e.g.* wood chopped up (1 Sam. vi. 14), eggs hatched (Isa. lix. 4), wild beasts rending (2 Kings ii. 24), of God's rending of rocks in the desert (Ps. lxxviii. 15). The one exception is Job xxviii. 10, where we have "he cutteth out rivers in the rocks," a curious difference from the preceding passage; there the accusative is צוּרִים, here it is יְאֹרִים, with בַּצּוּרוֹת following.

Such a rendering as (1) "The earth is rent (or, rends itself) into torrents," does obvious violence to the grammar; more especially as we have the Hithpael of this very verb found in this last meaning in a very apposite passage (Mic. i. 6). Much the same as this is Maurer's "flumina prorumpere jubet terra." As we have seen, there is no really parallel instance in the Piel. Maurer might have quoted Isa. xxxv. 6, where the Niphal is found of waters breaking forth, and Ps. lxxiv. 15, where the Kal is used in a corresponding active sense, but these do not affect the case of Piel. Again (2) we have Ewald's explanation, by which we get the idea, "Thou dost divide rivers so that there is now land where before was water." He compares Ps. cxiv. 5, 6, and Isa. xi. 15. Of course, so far as merely grammatical considerations go, this stands on exactly the same footing as the translation I argue for: "Thou dividest the land into rivers," and "Thou dividest the rivers so as to be land," being exact correlatives. Still, I must confess that for "dry land" as opposed to water, I should have expected יַבָּשָׁה rather than אֶרֶץ.

v. 10. In this verse the outcome of the Divine Presence is further described. The mountains, mightiest and most gigantic of the things of earth, see Him and tremble (lit., writhe) in awe, floods of rain pour down from the skies; the ocean, as though a being endued with life, utters his voice aloud, and tosses his hands on high.

It will be seen that the tense is now past, after shifting to the future at the Ethnakh of *v.* 8, of which change I have endeavoured to bring out the meaning as it presents itself to my mind. Here again is a change, the wonders of God's dealings in the past are a thought ever underlying the hopes for the future; and if *v.* 11 does indeed refer to the miracle in the Valley of Ajalon (and it is a view for which, as I believe, there is much to be said), then the general view is confirmed by the individual instance.[1]

By the word זֶרֶם may be understood violent rain, and עָבַר is clearly meant to emphasize its *excessive* and deluge-like character (*cf.* Isa. viii. 8, Nah. i. 8), as though "a deluge of waters poured overwhelmingly." The word is exclusively poetical, and save for the present passage and Job xxiv. 8 is found only in Isaiah.[2] We find it coupled with מָטָר (iv. 6), we have a זֶרֶם of hail (xxviii. 2), and accompanied by hail (xxx. 30). It is the violent downpour in the mountains upon the unsheltered outcasts (Job *l. c.*).

Ewald explains the clause differently, understanding it of the overflow of the waters of the Red Sea, after they had been parted for the passage of Israel, but now returning to their strength to engulf Israel's foes. Striking as is this idea, I do not see how it can fairly be reconciled with the meaning of זֶרֶם. Nor can it be maintained that the versions give any colour to this view. The LXX. is beside the mark, for it has utterly misunderstood the passage. The Targum (עֲנָנֵי מִטְרָא), and the Peshito (ܙܪܡܐ) are decided enough; and though the Vulgate (*turbo*) is not quite the same as this, it cannot be said to be materially different.[3]

---

[1] The tense of יָהֵל is clearly influenced by the tense of רָאוּךָ, as we have said above in the case of *v.* 7.

[2] iv. 6, xxv. 4 *bis*, xxviii. 2 *bis*, xxx. 30, xxxii. 2.

[3] We find *turbo* as the rendering of זֶרֶם in the Vulgate always, except in Isa. xxviii. 2, where it is *impetus*; in xxxii. 2, where it is *tempestas*; and in Job (*l. c.*), where it is *imbres*.

The Psalm of Habakkuk. 29

The noun רוֹם in the final clause is ordinarily taken as standing for an adverb, and this on the whole is perhaps the safest. If it be taken as the nominative to נָשָׂא, "the height lifted up its hands," it does not seem quite obvious what we are to understand by the "height." It has indeed been explained of the mountains, but the idea of the metaphor in this case seems far less natural and obvious than that of the tossing crests of the waves.

It must be allowed, however, that Jewish authorities have very generally taken רוֹם as the nominative. Thus the Targum understands it of the "powers of the height" who stand still in amaze (תְּמָהוּ קָמוּ). Rashi sees in תְּהוֹם and רוֹם the contrast between earth and heaven, "the inhabitants of the earth praised Him ... the hosts of the heaven lauded Him." Kimchi curiously explains it of the volume of the waters of the Jordan checked in their passage to the Dead Sea and forming a mighty heap (נֵד אֶחָד גָּבוֹהַּ). Aben Ezra also takes רוֹם as a nominative, the antithesis of תְהוֹם.

v. 11... שֶׁמֶשׁ. "Sun [and] moon stood still in[1] [their] abode." The ancient Jewish interpreters ordinarily understood this clause of the miracle wrought for Joshua at Gibeon. Thus the Targum has "when Thou didst work miracles for Joshua in the Valley of Gibeon, the sun and moon stood still in their habitations." So too it is explained by Rashi and Kimchi.[2] The latter says, "In the war of Joshua with the kings, when the sun stood still for them and the moon likewise, till the people should have avenged itself upon its enemies."

It may be noted further that in Joshua x. 13 we have this same verb twice used, "And the sun stood still (וַיִּדֹּם) and the moon stayed (עָמָד) .... And the sun stood still (וַיַּעֲמֹד) in the midst of heaven."

[1] For this modified use of the locative ה, see Böttcher, *Ausführliches Lehrbuch,* i. 629.
[2] Aben Ezra takes it differently. His view is that the sun and moon remained in their abode, because there was no need of the sun by day, nor of the moon by night, for "by the light of Thy arrows the sons of men are able to go about."

30   *The Psalm of Habakkuk.*

The fashion now prevails in Commentaries of giving a totally different interpretation: The sun and moon, so to speak, stayed at home; that is, either (1) they do not come forth from their dwelling (Ps. xix. 5, 6), *i.e.* do not rise; or (2) while in the sky they grow pale before the brightness of the Divine splendour (Ewald); or (3) the sun and moon are obscured by clouds "tonante et fulgurante cœlo" (Maurer).

If it be asked on what grounds the old traditional interpretation has been forsaken, it can but be said that a good many commentators contemptuously ignore it altogether. Or again, when reasons are given, they do not seem of a very cogent character, *e.g.* that עָמַד זְבֻלָה cannot possibly mean "stand still in the heavens," on which I can only remark that probably Rashi and Kimchi were quite as good judges of what Hebrew words could mean as *e.g.* Dr. Keil. Or again, that the "differences which exist between Josh. x. and Hab. iii. are too great for us to be able to allow that there is a reminiscence of Joshua in Habakkuk," which is simply to beg the whole question. When others again tell us that on this view it is impossible to find any connection between the two hemistichs of *v.* 11, it is sufficient to answer that the second hemistich brings before us the imagery of a terrible storm, in connection (as the succeeding context shows) with the idea of God as a warrior, avenging the cause of His people. Surely the words of Josh. x. 11, "the Lord cast down great stones from heaven," are suggestive of much not directly told, and might well shape the poetic imagery of the prophet.

It is of course entirely outside our province to discuss here the nature of the stupendous miracle at Gibeon; the question is merely as to the reference of Habakkuk. I venture to think that the old interpretation has by no means been disproved. In dwelling on the most striking wonders of the early history of Israel, in which such miracles as the passage of the Red Sea and the Jordan are confessedly referred to, in which again individual incidents such as the discomfiture of Midian and Cushan (whatever this latter may be) are brought in, why is it in any sense unnatural that the miracle of Gibeon should be thus

The Psalm of Habakkuk. 31

referred to?—and the rather that the victory in connection with which it was wrought was directly the turning-point in the conquest of the Holy Land.

The verb too, used by Habakkuk, is the same as one of the two used in Joshua, and is there applied both to sun and moon. Nor can it be said that such an idea, *e.g.* as either that of the sun obscured by thick clouds, or with its brightness paled by the presence of a greater splendour, can be very naturally expressed by a word meaning "stood still."

v. 11 ... לְאוֹר. The relative is of course to be understood before יְהַלֵּכוּ, the reference being to the arrows of God which fly abroad. The force of לְ will be "at" in the sense of "because of," if the view be taken of the dimming of the light of the sun and moon before the manifestation of God's glory. If, however, the reference to the victory in Gibeon be accepted, the לְ has more a local force "at," as though "amid" or "in the presence of."[1] The reference to "arrows" and "spear" gains additional point, if Josh. x. 11 (already referred to) be taken count of.

We may perhaps attempt to represent the force of the Piel by translating "by the light of thy fast-falling arrows."[2] The Piel of the verb הלך, which occurs in all 24 times in the Bible, is, save for one exception (1 Kings xxi. 27), found exclusively in the poetical books. The general aspect of the Piel in these cases, as indicating something more than the Kal, is that of permanence or continuance, the constant habit (see *e.g.* Pss. lxxxi. 14, lxxxvi. 11, lxxxix. 16). Except in Job xxiv. 10, this sense of continuousness in some sort seems to run more or less through all the passages (see further Eccl. iv. 15, viii. 10). Thus even in Lam. v. 18, it suggests the *unresting* running to and fro of the foxes amid the ruins of Zion. I do not think therefore that, having regard to this usage, we can treat the Piel now before us as suggestive of the swiftness of the lightning;

---

[1] So it is rendered נגד in a recent Rabbinic commentary.

[2] So the writer referred to in the preceding note remarks, חצים המהלכים בחוזק ולכן הוא בפעיל:

or that any similar idea enters into Ps. civ. 3. That verse seems to find its parallel in Nah. i. 3, and simply to mean that the mightiest powers of nature are God's servants. Thus in the present verse of Habakkuk we may understand the phrase of the ceaseless flashing of the lightning amid the discomfiture of Israel's foes.

v. 12. Here once again, for the last time in the Theophany, the prophet looks forward, and as before rests his certain belief of what is to come on the known deliverances of the past. Here, however, for the first time, the prophet dwells on the purpose of the Divine manifestation;[1] it was not merely for the destruction of the foe, for "Thou wentest forth for the salvation of Thy people."

The past tenses of *vv.* 13—15 might conceivably be instances of the prophetic perfect, but there is no need so to take them, and the general scope of our view of the Theophany which ends with *v.* 15 is thus consistently maintained. Let it be noted too that the Theophany is thus made to end with a definite reference to that deliverance of old which was the closest parallel to that from the Chaldæans, namely that from Egypt. The reference in *v.* 15 to the passage of the Red Sea certainly seems unmistakeable, and it is so understood by Ewald, who sees a reference to Pharaoh and Egypt all through the paragraph *vv.* 13—15.

v. 13. אֶת־מְשִׁיחֶךָ. We are faced here with a twofold difficulty, on which it is well to speak with caution, the meaning of the particle and the reference to the "Anointed." If the particle means *with*, then the reference is clearly to our Lord, as the worker out of God's purposes of salvation. This view is taken by the Vulgate, and by other ancient versions to be subsequently referred to, and is strongly advocated by Dr. Pusey (*comm. in loc.*). He points out with justice that if the את be objective, then, in face of the foregoing clause, it is a superfluity, and there was no reason for changing the construction. On the other hand we are bound to admit that the translation "with Thy

---

[1] That is, by explicit statement; for we have already had the implied hint in יְשׁוּעָה, *v.* 8.

The Psalm of Habakkuk. 33

Anointed" introduces a fresh thought in the poem, where God is directly brought before us as the deliverer and avenger.

If, on the other hand, the particle be objective, it then becomes a question as to the reference in "Thy Anointed." It may perhaps be the nation, that is, in the higher sense, not "Israel after the flesh," but the "Israel of God"; or it may be understood in varying senses as the Anointed King of Israel.

On turning to the ancient versions, we find that great diversity of view prevails. The Targum and Peshito, while clearly taking the particle as objective, have left the further point indeterminate. The LXX. again, while taking the objective, has readings τὸν χριστὸν and τοὺς χριστούς, the latter taking the Hebrew word in a collective sense, and presumably referring to the people of Israel. Jerome (comm. in loc.) comments on the renderings of the other Greek versions. We learn that Aquila rendered the clause "for salvation (i.e. to Thy people) with Thy Christ" (sing.). The same is also the rendering of the Quinta. Theodotion ("quasi pauper Ebionita") and Symmachus ("ejusdem dogmatis"), both "pauperem sensum secuti," render "to save thy Christ" (sing.). Jerome, who, as I have already said, takes the את as meaning *with*, as Aquila does, expresses his surprise, "Isti semichristiani Judaice transtulerunt, et Judæus Aquila interpretatus est ut Christianus." Lastly, the *Sexta* gives a distinctly Christian interpretation, ἐξῆλθες τοῦ σῶσαι τὸν λαόν σου διὰ Ἰησοῦν τὸν Χριστόν σου.

Of Rabbinic commentaries, Rashi explains the "Anointed" of Saul and David, Aben Ezra of the King of Judah, and Kimchi of Messiah the Son of David.

If the view be taken that the particle is objective, it is by no means easy to decide between the people of Israel, defined as above, and the King of Israel; but I am not convinced that the arguments urged against the former view are conclusive. Specially is it pointed out that we never find the people of Israel called by this name "Anointed" in scripture; and certainly the passages adduced are by no means free from doubt. Still, to assert that they all (Pss. xxviii. 8, lxxxiv. 10, lxxxix. 39) *must* refer to the anointed king, and Ps. cv. 15 to the Patriarchs,

3

comes very near to begging the point at issue. I confess that, as regards the first three passages, I should have thought that the question was a very open one, where either view might very fairly be maintained. Now, in the passage of Habakkuk, if "the Anointed" be a king, we may ask, what king? In answer, we are told, "Not this or that historical king, Josiah, Jehoiakim, nor yet Jehoiachin, but the Davidic king absolutely, including the Messiah," the last and most glorious of the line. But to this it may fairly be answered that (1) it assumes as absolutely certain that the past tense יָצָאתָ is a *prophetic* perfect, which anyhow may be considered as open to doubt; (2) as regards the former part of the above view, this notion of the Davidic king is simply a piece of vague idealising, which, we venture to think, could have no place in a prophecy, for God did not save any one king of the line of David from the Chaldæans; and (3) the inclusion of Him who is *the* Messiah seems to introduce a very questionable piece of theology. The נוֹשָׁע of Zech. ix. 9, which is quoted in support of this view, may most simply be translated *victorious* or *fortunate*.

If, however, as we believe, the past tenses of this verse are really past tenses, then the deliverances may easily find examples drawn from the past history; nor does it matter very much whether we understand the "Anointed" of the king or the nation, for the former is but the representative of the latter. Further, we cannot afford too lightly to reject the other view of the clause, which does not view אֵת as the objective prefix. It is indeed even conceivable that the seeming ambiguity was intentional.

In the second half of the verse we turn from considering those whom God defends to those on whom He works vengeance. The "wicked one," primarily of course the hostile king, as representative of his people, is doubtless to be understood of every successive embodiment of evil. The metaphor of the verse is that of a stronghold, where the Divine Power strikes at once at the summit and the foundation. The pinnacle is dashed off and the foundation laid bare (*cf.* Ps. cxxxvii. 7).

I must confess to feeling not content with the ordinary ways of explaining the last clause. Thus Gesenius (*Thesaurus*, p. 1162) renders the clause, " ædificia ad hominis altitudinem diruuntur." But this is not altogether fair treatment of the Hebrew. To "lay bare the foundations" is of course tantamount to the destruction of the building, but then "to the neck" should surely be understood in a way directly harmonising with the original phrase. Ewald explains the phrase as of the building decapitated, so to speak, by the dashing off of the head, so that the neck is laid bare. Then from this now highest point, the neck, to the very foundation, is the building shattered. This is the view taken in the Peshito. Still, vivid as this idea is, it may be objected that thus to treat the word יְסוֹד as to all intents and purposes "from the very foundations" is rather questionable grammar.

Now, a comparison of Isa. viii. 8, xxx. 28, shows that the phrase עַד צַוָּאר is used by a metaphor taken from the human body, to imply an overwhelming flood in which life is in deadly peril; the body is well nigh entirely submerged. Here, however, we are not dealing with rising waters, but with digging down to the foundations of a building. Might we then not argue, by parity of reason, that the foundation is laid bare to the lowest stone thereof.

v. 14. Here and in *v*. 15, with which the Theophany closes, the thought is continued of the mighty works done in the time of the fathers, culminating in the passage of the Red Sea.

In the first clause of *v*. 14 we meet with a word occurring nowhere else in Scripture, whose meaning, though most probably that of "chieftains" or "leaders," cannot be considered altogether free from doubt. The root-meaning underlying this word פרזו (פְּרָזָיו *Krî*) is not so completely established as to settle the matter satisfactorily. Parallel instances, as we have said, there are none; and while we may probably associate the word with פְּרָזוֹן (Judg. v. 7, 11), it is impossible to allow that this word will settle the matter, in face of the existence of פְּרָזִי and פְּרָזָה in a totally different sense.

It must be allowed that a suitable meaning is obtained from

either translation, "Thou didst pierce with his[1] spears the head of his chieftains," or "the head of his hordes (swarms of invaders)"; but I cannot but think that there is insufficient evidence for this latter view, where the meaning is deduced from a word which simply means an inhabitant of an unwalled town (paganus). Nor can it be said that anything *conclusive* for this view can be obtained from the versions. The LXX. has δυνάσται, and the Peshito adopts the same view. The Vulgate has *bellatores*, and the Targum, which sees in this verse a reference to the discomfiture of Pharaoh, has גיברי רישי משרית. These last two, however, seem almost too vague to prove very much.

Rashi, who understands the verse of the invading army of Sennacherib and the destruction which befell it, does indeed connect the word with the second-named meaning, "the chiefs of his cities and his towns." Kimchi also, who takes the past tenses as instances of the prophetic perfect, sees a reference to the future wars of Gog, and explains the פְּרָזָיו as his hosts (חייליותיו), which dwelt in the villages round about Jerusalem.

Delitzsch refers the word to an absolute singular form פֶּרָז or פְּרָז, and, dealing as we are with an ἅπαξ λεγόμενον, it is clearly impossible to dogmatise between these and פְּרָז, the form generally taken. He explains the word "der Dorf- und Bauerschaft," and appeals to the Targum, Rashi, and Kimchi in support of his view. The two latter certainly held this view; the Targum seems to me open to doubt.

It must be allowed that the word יִסְעֲרוּ is a very natural expression for the fierce rush of invading hordes, but the evidence before us seems perhaps hardly sufficient to allow us to accept without question this rendering. For the present it may be well to follow the advice of the Talmud, and "teach our tongues to say, we do not know."

---

[1] The pronoun "his" clearly refers to the רָשָׁע of the foregoing verse. Ewald would prefer to read מַטָּיו, thinking "his" awkward here; but, if retained, as meaning "spears destined for the wicked." I should have thought it might equally well have been explained of the foe's own spears, turned against himself. *Cf.* 2 Chron. xx. 23 sqq.

The Psalm of Habakkuk. 37

Be the meaning of the word what it may, the imagery brings before us the whirlwind like rush of the foes of Israel, the future יִסְעֲרוּ presumably indicating the way in which mass after mass of invaders pour on, "velut unda supervenit undam." These invaders in the wild exultation of their onset are like bandits, whose joy is to pillage, and as it were devour, the wretched traveller whom they have drawn into their secret haunts.[1]

The spears of the enemy are turned against themselves, and the onward rush is stayed by the might of Israel's protector.

v. 15. With this verse the Theophany comes to an end, and that, as we believe, with a reference to the miracle of the passage of the Red Sea.

A most striking parallel to this verse is found in Ps. lxxvii. 20, where the thought underlying the whole context is very relevant to much in the present poem, "Thy way is in the sea and thy paths in mighty waters, and thy footsteps are not known." So in Habakkuk we read, "Thou didst march across the sea with[2] thy horses, the foaming mass of mighty waters." With this reminiscence of the great deliverance, when the then mightiest empire of earth was discomfited and forced to surrender its captives, the prophet ends. It is an end recalling the beginning. The God who of old led his people through the desert like a flock, and wrought mightily for them, was the God of Israel still; He would again in anger tread the earth, and in fury trample down the nations, even He who once subdued the pride of the sea, and marched as a conqueror over the foaming mass[3] of mighty waters.

---

[1] We may note the affix in לַהֲפִיצֵנִי, where the prophet identifies himself with the victims of the invasion.

[2] The סוּסֶיךָ is simply taken as depending on an implied בְּ, and there is clearly no need to imply דַּרְכּוֹ after it.

[3] This word חֹמֶר does not occur again in the Bible in *exactly* this sense, though we find it used (as in Exod. viii. 10, Job xxvii. 16) for a "heap" in other senses. Still, the use of the verb חמר in Ps. xlvi. 4 fully justifies the translation "a foaming mass of waters." The Vulgate gives *lutum*, a meaning which, while fairly representing the word, *e.g.* in Gen. xi. 3, is entirely out of place here.

38   *The Psalm of Habakkuk.*

v. 16. Here, the Theophany ended, the prophet reappears more distinctly in his own personality, as in *v.* 2. The news he has to declare excites in his own heart mingled feelings of awe and thankfulness, or, rather should we say, the feeling of alarm and dread, called forth by the thought of the impending ruin of the nation, pales before the knowledge that beneath and beyond all this is the unchanging love of God for His people. The word on which the change of thought hinges is clearly אָנוּחַ, in which we seem to turn from the mere terror[1] of the first clause of the verse, to the fixed hope and exultation, in spite of all circumstances of gloom and distress, which animate the following verses.

The second hemistich of the verse is not free from grammatical difficulty; some doubt exists as to the way in which we should translate the word אֲשֶׁר. Noldius (*Conc. Part. Heb.* p. 102 *a*) renders it by *yet* (tamen); for this he gives no parallel instance in Scripture, and I do not think that this meaning can be at all substantiated. Subsequently (not. 550), he enumerates several other views, none of which can be considered satisfactory.[2] Thus we have (1) *quamvis*,[3] for which (p. 100) the references Num. xii. 11, Eccl. viii. 12,[4] 2 Sam. iv. 10, are given. But in the first of these the אֲשֶׁר is clearly the relative, used as a cognate accusative; in the second, the meaning of *because* may very reasonably be taken; and in the third, אֲשֶׁר is certainly a relative, referring to the messenger.

---

[1] So enthralling is the prophet's terror, that it is as though the body itself must dissolve before thoughts so terrible: "Rottenness begins to enter into my bones," the future being used, as often, as a true imperfect.

[2] His remark, "absque אֲשֶׁר LXX. ἀναπαύσομαι," is incorrect, because in some way or other, the אֲשֶׁר has ἡ ἕξις μου underlying it.

[3] Gesenius remarks (*Thes.* p. 165 *b*) "raro est concedentis; *etsi*," and gives as his sole example Eccl. viii. 10.

[4] The general sense of *v.* 11 is clearly that sinners, because they sin with impunity, think God's long suffering is simply indifference (2 Pet. iii. 9); the אֲשֶׁר at the beginning of the verse meaning *because*. But if, with Mendelssohn, we take (*v.* 12) the מֵאֲרִיךְ of God, with an ellipsis of אַף, the same will hold good here, "Because a sinner sins a hundred times, yet God still has long suffering towards him."

The Psalm of Habakkuk.

Again (2) the meaning *certe* is proposed, though I do not think that this would give a very convenient sense to the passage in Habakkuk. The examples given by Noldius are the following, some of which at any rate are more than questionable: (*a*) Eccl. i. 10, (*b*) 1 Sam. xv. 20, (*c*) Zech. viii. 23, (*d*) Job ix. 15, (*e*) Isa. v. 28, (*f*) Isa. viii. 20. In (*a*), however, אֲשֶׁר is undoubtedly a relative, whose antecedent is עוֹלָמִים, the nominative with a false concord to הָיָה; in (*b*) we have merely a sign which introduces an *oratio recta*, like ὅτι; in (*c*) and (*f*) the particle simply indicates the apodosis of the sentence; in (*e*) certainly, and in (*d*) most probably, אֲשֶׁר is a relative. However, whether this last-named meaning be established or not, and this may be doubted, it does not, as we have said, seem to fit well into our present passage.

Yet again (3) some would take it as *utinam*; so Luther (O dass ich ruhen möchte), on which and on others Noldius justly remarks, " Egregie, si significationes illæ sunt usitatæ."

Another view, which is perfectly compatible with grammar and which is frequently taken here, is to take the אֲשֶׁר as "in that," "because." The objection to this seems to me to lie in the meaning of אָנוּחַ, which is not simply "to wait." If it were, the sense would be plain, " I tremble where I stand, because I must await, there being no escape, the day of calamity that approaches." Still, the root נוּח hardly means this, or rather it means much more; it is not the trembling waiting for an irrevocable doom, but the calm, patient acceptance of that doom, the courage which accepts the inevitable, but regards it with peaceful unruffled composure. It is the heroic calm of Gordon waiting for the end at Khartoum, or the peaceful composure of Bishop Ridley, which could enable him to sleep tranquilly on the night before his fiery martyrdom.

Thus I believe that אֲשֶׁר may best be taken as the simple relative, " I who will patiently and silently wait for the day of trouble."[1] This יוֹם צָרָה is then further defined; it is the

---

[1] The general thought of the expression reminds one of the דּוּמִיָּה נַפְשִׁי (Ps. lxii. 2); and the לְ after אֱמוּנָה of the similar construction Isa. xli. 1.

invasion of the Chaldæan foe, "even for the coming up against [the][1] people of him who shall invade him in troops (or assail him)." The לְ of לַעֲלוֹת is parallel to and exegetical of that of לְיוֹם, and עַם, in spite of the absence of the article, is clearly equivalent to הָעָם or עַמִּי. If this be assumed, then the subject of יְגוּדֶנּוּ, before which we may supply an אֲשֶׁר, will be the Chaldæans pouring in with their hosts.

vv. 17—19. We have said that the word אָנוּחַ gives the clue to the transition of thought. Amid all the calamities that will[2] attend the invasion, amid devastation and havoc, with utter desolation where once was a very garden of Eden, the prophet will *rest*. He will rest, because, in spite of all, he is able to rejoice in God his Saviour, and knows that He is his strength and protection.

[1] The absence of the article here, where it would seem logically necessary, may be paralleled by לְקֹל in the same verse.

[2] The future tense תִּפְרַח clearly influences the whole verse; the disasters are yet to come, though in the later verbs the undoubted event is viewed as really come, and the prophet, like an apocalyptic seer, gazes upon the actual desolation.

CHAPTER II.

THE SEPTUAGINT VERSION OF THE PSALM.

It is much to be regretted that the amount of help to be got from the Septuagint for either the criticism or exegesis of this Psalm is almost nil. The difficulties of the poem were evidently far beyond the powers of the translator to cope with them; the general scope and drift of the poem were certainly very faintly perceived by him, and the subtle delicacies of thought, in which, in spite of the exceeding differences between the two languages, much might have been achieved by a competent translator, are as a whole impartially slurred over.

When to this we must add the existence of a large crop of absolute and palpable blunders, and also a perceptible element of corruption of text, it is evident that a translation with such a record is one which can only be used with the utmost caution as an exponent of the difficulties of the Psalm.

The Masoretic text may not indeed be absolutely faultless; but, thanks to the reverent care which has been lavished on it, we believe that we have in all essentials (nay probably with but the slightest imperfections) the true text of this wonderful poem; while this, its most ancient translation, is but a poor travesty, like a blundering schoolboy's exercise.

Thus work on the Greek text of the Psalm must turn largely on an examination of the curious mistranslations of which it is full, and of the corruptions of the text. Even blunders, however, more than two thousand years old, become venerable; and all the more when it is remembered how almost entirely Old Testament exegesis in the early Christian Church rested upon the Septuagint, till Jerome brought a higher learning to bear. The exposition of this Psalm in the *de Civitate Dei*[1] of Augustine

---

[1] xviii. 32.

furnishes an instance of eloquent spiritual teaching, where the premises are often absolutely untenable.[1]

[All the readings cited from the three great uncials have been verified,—in the case of A from the autotype, and in those of אB from the editions of Tischendorf and of Vercellone and Cozza respectively. The Complutensian and Aldine texts have been cited, so far as it seemed necessary. The evidence of the cursives, when given, is taken from Holmes and Parsons. Four of these may be specially referred to (Codd. 23, 62, 86, 147) as giving us a totally different translation, which keeps on the whole fairly close to the Hebrew.[2] One of these (Cod. 86), a Barberini MS., was known to Montfaucon, who says of it (*Hexapl.* ii. 377): "Esse vero Septimam Editionem vix est quod dubitemus," and cites it throughout the chapter as ἄλλος.

Two versions of the LXX. have been steadily kept in view throughout, the Old Latin and the Syro-Hexaplaric. In cases of citation from the latter, the text, as given by Middeldorpf, has been verified by comparison with the photo-lithographic reproduction of Dr. Ceriani.

The Latin has, however, in one sense, a higher interest than the Syriac, quite apart from its value as a translation, from the way in which it entered both into the theology and liturgies of the Western Church.

For the Old Latin of this Psalm, I have mainly relied on the text given by Sabatier (which is that embodied in Jerome's Com-

[1] Take as an example a comment on *v.* 2, "*Montem umbrosum atque condensum*, quamvis multis modis possit intelligi, libentius acceperim Scripturarum altitudinem divinarum, quibus prophetatus est Christus." Or, on *vv.* 6. 7, "*Ingressus æternos ejus pro laboribus vidi;* hoc est, non sine mercede æternitatis laborem caritatis vidi."

[2] This remark applies to Habakkuk iii. only. Both in the rest of Habakkuk and in the prophets generally the text of the four cursives is simply that of the LXX. The last three constantly, but by no means invariably, agree together (Cod. 23 often differing), and they frequently display, some or all of them, a markedly correct text. I may take as illustrations the following cases, where the Roman text is certainly corrupt: Hos. iii. 1, omit μετὰ (23); x. 13, ἅρμασι (all); xiii. 3, καπνοδοχῆς (23), ἀκρίδων (the rest). Amos i. 11, μήτραν (86); viii. 6, om. καὶ *prim.* (62, 147). Micah i. 14, δώσεις (all), 16, ξήρησιν, clearly an itacism for ξύρησιν (all but 23): vi. 7, χειμαρρῶν (147). Hab. i. 13, οὐ ἐυνήσῃ (or ει), (all but 23).

The Septuagint Version of the Psalm. 43

mentary on Habakkuk), and the readings cited by him. I have also had regard to the text given by Cardinal Thomasius in his *Psalterium cum Canticis*,[1] to that contained in the Mozarabic Breviary,[2] and to a small portion found in the Roman Missal.[3] In addition to these is the text contained in the exposition of Augustine referred to above.

Lastly, an examination has been made of all citations of the Psalm in the Ante-Nicene Fathers, Greek and Latin, though it cannot be said that anything of importance has been yielded therefrom.]

v. 1. μετὰ ᾠδῆς. For this translation of שִׁגָּיוֹן, reference may be made to the preceding chapter.

v. 2. I believe the original reading of the first two clauses to have been, Κύριε, εἰσακήκοα τὴν ἀκοήν σου· Κύριε,[4] κατενόησα τὰ ἔργα σου. Thus יָרֵאתִי is treated as though it were רָאִיתִי[5]; and the [καὶ] ἐφοβήθην[6] and [καὶ] ἐξέστην are duplicate renderings of יָרֵאתִי, with its proper spelling.

Again, to obtain the next two clauses, we must treat the Hebrew as if it were בְּקֶרֶב שָׁנַיִם חַיֵּיהוּ, בְּקֶרֶב שָׁנִים תּוֹדִיעַ׃ The γνωσθήσῃ is of course a duplicate with ἐπιγνωσθήσῃ, which has been put in where it has no business.

Moreover, the clauses ἐν τῷ ἐγγίζειν τὰ ἔτη ἐπιγνωσθήσῃ, and ἐν τῷ παρεῖναι τὸν καιρὸν[7] ἀναδειχθήσῃ are duplicates, the second being clearly the earlier. The Syro-Hexaplaric obelizes ἐν τῷ παρεῖναι .... τὴν ψυχήν μου.[8]

---

[1] pp. 694 sqq.
[2] Here it forms the Canticle at Lauds on the 3rd Sunday in Advent.
[3] *vv.* 2, 3, occur as a *Tractus* on Good Friday.
[4] The second Κύριε is omitted by AB. It is found, however, in א, in 19 of Holmes and Parsons' cursives, in the Complutensian and Aldine editions, and in the Syro-Hexaplaric version. It is also found in the verse as cited by Origen (*de Orat. Libellus*, c. 14; Vol. XVII. 144, ed. Lommatzsch) and others, and is manifestly genuine.
[5] κατανοέω often stands for רָאָה, see Gen. xlii. 9; Exod. ii. 11, xix. 21; Num. xxxii. 8, 9; Isa. v. 12.
[6] εὐλαβήθην, Codd. 62, 86, 147.
[7] עֵת is rendered by καιρὸς in Jud. x. 8 (Cod. B).
[8] The whole is, however, cited by Irenæus (iii. 16. 7).

In the remaining clause of the verse, ἐν τῷ ταραχθῆναι τὴν ψυχήν μου and ἐν ὀργῇ ἐλέους are duplicates, the former being the older. רגז is treated as though an infinitive construct,[1] and רחם as though רוחי.[2]

It cannot be doubted that in the mind of the original translator, the δύο ζῶα of this verse were the Cherubim overshadowing the Mercy-seat (see Exod. xxv. 22, Num. vii. 89), and so it is understood, *e.g.* by Theodoret (*de S. Trin. Dial.* i., Vol. v. 943, ed. Schulze and Noesselt). Various other interpretations, however, have been put forth by various Fathers, all alike impossible as an exegesis of the true meaning of the passage.

Tertullian (*adv. Marc.* iv. 22) takes the δύο ζῶα to be Moses and Elias, and sees in the passage a reference to our Lord's Transfiguration. Augustine (*de Civ. Dei* xviii. 32), besides the above, suggests also the two Testaments and the two thieves; and Jerome (*comm. in loc.*) adds yet other views.

One other interpretation may be noted as curious, the view which understands the two animals of the Ox and the Ass standing by the manger in which the Saviour was laid. See Tillemont, *Mémoires*, i. 447 (Note 5, "*Sur le bœuf et l'asne de la Crèche*"), and the illustrations given in Smith and Cheetham's *Dict. of Christian Antiquities*, *s. v. Nativity, The, in Art.*

We may remark lastly that certain Fathers have stated, or implied, that the reading should be, not δύο ζώων, but δύο ζωῶν, "two lives." (So Euseb. *Dem. Ev.* l. vi., c. 15, § 4; Cyr. Hier. *Cat.* xii., c. 20; see also Origen, *de Princip.* i. 4, Vol. XXI. 75). The "two lives" are explained (Cyril, *l. c.*) of our Lord's life before His resurrection and after it, and in other ways.

v. 3. κατασκίου δασέος (δασέως Aא). It can hardly be doubted that we must view this as a duplicate rendering, or rather pair of duplicates, of פָּארָן. As is not surprising in such a case of conflation, several texts omit different individual renderings. Thus fifteen cursives, the Aldine and the Syro-Hexaplaric, and some texts of the Old Latin, omit Φαράν, the

---

[1] ταράσσειν stands for רגז in this chapter, *v.* 16.

[2] See Gen. xli. 8; Exod. xxxv. 21.

The Septuagint Version of the Psalm. 45

Complutensian and three cursives omit δασέος, and three cursives[1] omit κατασκίου δασέος. Irenæus (iii. 20. 4) has simply "de monte Effrem," but the same Father (iv. 33. 11) "de monte umbroso et condenso."

As to the manner in which this curious rendering has been obtained, several suggestions have been made, which can hardly be possible. Such are the views that the Greek is a corruption of διασκεδάσεως, representing some noun derived from פור or פרר; or of ἐξ ὄρους δόξης, i.e. פְּאֵר. Hardly more reasonable is the view that κατασκίου and δασέος are two translations of פְּאֵרָה or פֹּארָה, read mistakenly for פָּארָן.[2]

I venture to suggest the following as at any rate possible. The word κατάσκιος occurs elsewhere three times: (1) for רַעֲנָן (of a tree), Jer. ii. 20; (2) for עֲבוֹת[3] (of trees), Ezek. xx. 28; (3) for מְצוּלָה (of mountains), Zech. i. 8.[4] Again, δασύς stands for עֲבוֹת (of trees), Lev. xxiii. 40, Neh. viii. 15; for עֲבֻתָּה (of an oak), Ezek. vi. 13; for רַעֲנָן (of trees), Deut. xii. 2, Isa. lvii. 5; and for שָׂעִיר or שֵׂעָר (of a hairy man), Gen. xxv. 25, xxvii. 11, 23; 4 Kings i. 8. From the common ground in all this, it will clearly appear how completely κατάσκιος and δασύς are akin in their usage.

Now if our present passage be compared with Deut. xxxiii. 2 and Judges v. 4, 5, we find in all alike the same imagery as to the Manifestation of God's glory. In the former of the two parallels, Sinai, Seir, and Mount Paran are associated, and in the latter, Seir, Edom, and Sinai. Yet all three passages show that we must look for some deeper idea of association than a geographical one, for Seir and Sinai are far apart. Teman is a district or city of Edom, and therefore to be asssociated with Edom. Paran, of course, may be used generally of the great

[1] This is perhaps not strictly relevant, as the three cursives are, Codd. 62, 86, 147.
[2] So Agellius, p. 144.
[3] It is worth noting the one other rendering of נֹצָה, σύσκιος (of trees) Ezek. vi. 13.
[4] The ההדסים of the Heb. has been misread as הֶהָרִים in the LXX.

wilderness of Paran, but it is more probable that it refers to some individual height in the Sinaitic peninsula. In any case names are used in the present passage which a comparison of the two other passages justifies us in viewing as being, if not geographically, yet at any rate in recognised poetic imagery, cognate with Seir. The name of this mountain means "rough" or "shaggy," and, whatever may be the case now, it would be fitly applied to hills covered with trees and bushes, rather than to hills rough or rugged in a more general sense. There is also a neighbouring line of hills, "Mount Halak" (Josh. xi. 17), i.e. "smooth" or "bare." The two adjectives שָׂעִיר and חָלָק are used to distinguish Esau and Jacob.

Now if Paran or Teman were viewed in poetic imagery as virtually the same with Seir, then, the meaning of this last name being what it is, κατάσκιος and δασύς might well have been descriptive epithets, possibly at first marginal remarks, ultimately finding their way into the text.

Before leaving this passage, it is perhaps worth noting a curious translation of ἐκ Θαιμάν found in some texts of the Old Latin, a Libano. This occurs e.g. in the text of Card. Thomasius, and in those contained in the Mozarabic Breviary and the Roman Missal. So also Greg. Magn. *Moral.* xxxiii. 1. Thomasius suggests that it is an error for *a Libanoto*. Rather should it be *a Libonoto*, i.e. ἀπὸ λιβονότου. There does not, it is true, seem to be any trace of this reading, but the three cursives, Codd. 62, 86, 147, read ἀπὸ λιβός.

v. 3. ἀρετή. This stands for הוֹד also in Zech. vi. 13. For this our four cursives read ἡ εὐπρέπεια [or τὴν εὐπ.] τῆς δόξης αὐτοῦ.

v. 4. ἔθετο is simply שָׂם for שָׁם.[1]

— ἀγάπησιν treats חֶבְיוֹן "covert" from the root חבה, חבא, as though from חבב or אהב.[2]

---

[1] The reading of the "four cursives" ἐπεστήρικται [ἀπεστήρικται, Cod. 23] is presumably due to the same cause.

[2] Presumably the latter; for on the one occurrence of the *verb* חבב (Deut. xxxiii. 2), it is rendered ἐφείσατο; whereas in more than 150 instances ἀγαπάω represents אהב. Also in all the seven instances where ἀγάπησις occurs in the canonical books, it represents אַהֲבָה.

The Septuagint Version of the Psalm. 47

v. 4. κραταιὰν is in duplicate with ἰσχύος αὐτοῦ, as though עֻזֹּה.

v. 5. λόγος is of course דָּבָר in place of דֶּבֶר. Here the four cursives read πτῶσις, which represents the Masoretic pointing.

— πεδία is presumably due to a different division of the letters, הֹשׁפֵל|וּרְגָלָיו See *e.g.* Deut. i. 7. It has been suggested that πεδία represents שִׁפִי, which view has the advantage of leaving the לְ to represent the κατά; but this word is never rendered πεδία in the LXX.[1]

The curious error εἰς παιδείαν has entered into no less than seventeen cursive MSS., besides the Aldine text. Theodoret also (*Int. in Psal.* 84; Vol. I. 1208) has this reading, on which he comments.

Some have suggested, most needlessly, that πεδία is a corruption of πετεινά. The four cursives, already mentioned as having so individual a text, do indeed read τὰ μέγιστα τῶν πετεινῶν, but the rendering πετεινά is simply due to an altogether independent view as to the meaning of רֶשֶׁף, and agrees with the rendering of the Peshito in the present passage.[2] So too Aquila appears to have read πτηνόν (*volatile*, Jerome), and Symmachus, Theodotion, and the Quinta, πετεινόν (*volucrem*, id.). Again, in the well-known verse of Job (v. 7), "Man is born unto trouble, as the sparks fly upwards," the רֶשֶׁף is by some authorities rendered "young birds."[3] We are not now concerned to discuss the correctness of this view; it is sufficient to say that it was current.[4] It is quite clear, however, that the existing text of the LXX. has had an altogether different origin.

---

[1] Still, נִשְׁפָּה is rendered πεδινόν, Isa. xiii. 2.

[2] As also in Job v. 7, but not in Ps. lxxvii. 48 (lxxviii. Heb.).

[3] So Aquila, υἱοὶ πτηνοῦ; Symmachus, τὰ τέκνα τῶν πετεινῶν; and the LXX., νεοσσοὶ γυπός. So also in Psalm (*l. c.*), where, though the LXX. has πυρί, Symm. has οἰωνοῖς, and Aquila, it would seem, πετεινοῖς.

[4] There seems no need to appeal to Arabic to get the necessary root-meaning; that of "flash" is sufficient. We may compare Tennyson's

" . . . the curlews call,
Dreary *gleams* about the moorland."

48   *The Septuagint Version of the Psalm.*

v. 6. ἐσαλεύθη. The derivation of יִמֹדֶד from מדד gives a somewhat tame sense "he measured"; and the view of the LXX., which implies a root מוד, akin to מוט, seems to be more to the point.[1] It should be noted that there is no second case of the Poel of מדד in the Bible. Further, the existence of the Piel מִדֵּד in the sense of *measuring*, is an objection to the existence of the Poel in the same sense. Moreover, the Targum, which renders אָזִיע, takes the same view as the LXX.

— διετάκη [וַיַּתֵּר]. This is simply due to a confusion between נתר and נתך. See Ezek. xxiv. 11; Nah. i. 6.

The "four cursives," together with the Complutensian, read here ἐξείκασε (or ἐξήκασε). It is suggested in Schleusner's *Lexicon* (*s.v.* ἐξεικάζω) that this is an error for ἐξέτηξε. I must confess that this does not strike me as at all probable. If there were a corruption of text, it would be more reasonable to suggest ἐξετίναξε, which stands for נתר in 2 Sam. xxii. 33, Dan. iv. 11. Obviously, however, there has been simply a confusion with וַיָּתַר, from the root תור, "to search out, or investigate"; and εἰκάζω is found in this sense in Jer. xxvi. 43 [xlvi. 23, Heb.].[2]

— ἐτάκησαν [שָׁחוּ]. This translation has doubtless been obtained through a confusion with the Chaldee root שיח (liquefactus est). See Exod. xvi. 21 (*Targ. Ps. Jon.* and *Jerushalmi*). So also in Syriac, Wisd. xvi. 27; 2 Pet. iii. 12.

— βίᾳ [עַד, perpetuity]. The simplest change is to suppose a confusion with עֹז, taken adverbially.[3]

— πορείας αἰωνίας αὐτοῦ. This accusative must presumably be understood as an accusative of reference, "in view of His goings."[4] We might compare the common use of φοβεῖσθαι

[1] The "four cursives," which read διεμέτρησεν, refer the word to the former root.

[2] If another suggestion is sought, one might propose ἐξήτασε, from ἐξετάζω in the above sense, but this is unnecessary.

[3] For τὰ ὄρη, our four cursives read αἱ νάπαι, which also represents גבעה in Isa. xl. 12; see also Song iv. 6 (Symm.).

[4] The Syro-Hexaplaric makes it simpler by prefixing to "goings" the preposition ܠ.

with the accusative, which in strictness would be "to feel internal alarm in view of" this or that object. Thus here, "the eternal hills melted before His-eternal goings." ἐτάκησαν would thus be a more vivid and pictorial equivalent for ἐφοβήθησαν.

v. 7. ἀντὶ κόπων (πόνων in the Complutensian). What the translators understood by their own Greek, or whether indeed it conveyed any very definite meaning, may perhaps be doubted, and one can readily understand the diversity of interpretation that has arisen. Jerome's view (*comm. in loc.*), which applies alike to the Hebrew and the Greek, has been already mentioned. It amounts to this, that men who devote their lives to the acquisition of gain and to base pursuits become the abode of demons instead of being the Temples of God. Augustine (*de Civ. Dei*, xviii. 32) punctuates the words differently, "Ingressus æternos eius pro laboribus vidi,"[1] and it is worth noting that Cod. A of the LXX. has the colon after αἰώνιοι, and not at the end of the verse; though of course, from the standpoint of the Hebrew, such a grouping is impossible. Augustine's interpretation of the clause is "non sine mercede æternitatis laborem caritatis aspexi."

In the Latin text of Jerome the πορείας has been viewed as a genitive ("Colles sæculi itineris sempiterni ejus"), which recalls Hitzig's view as to the Hebrew, referred to in the preceding chapter. The form in the Mozarabic Breviary goes more widely afield, "itinera sæcularia ejus pro laboribus. Viderunt...," though the cause of the blunder is obvious.

In the Psalter of Thomasius and other Latin texts we have "præ (not *pro*) laboribus." This, however, though giving a striking sense, has been clearly altered from a text which read *pro*.

— καὶ αἱ σκηναὶ. The καὶ αἱ is suspicious. There is nothing in the Hebrew calling for καὶ, and its position after the verb is awkward; also the article before σκηναὶ might very well be left out according to Septuagintal usage, due to the Hebrew

[1] So too the Cod. S. Germ. and others cited by Sabatier.

idiom, and so the σκηνώματα in the preceding clause. When further we find that thirteen cursives and the Aldine omit the αἰ, one cursive the καὶ, and three cursives the καὶ αἰ, I think that it is quite possible that the two words are due to a sort of dittographia with the last syllable of the preceding word.[1]

v. 9. ἐνέτεινας. The past tense is read by Codd. אB, but Aא^{ca, cb}, one other uncial MS. (xii. of Holmes and Parsons), twenty-one cursives, and the Aldine read the future ἐντενεῖς. The latter reading, which is called for by the Hebrew, is also that of Origen (*Sel. in Threnos*; Vol. XIII. 190).

The translation is of course not literal, but is a very obvious Midrash. The "baring" of the bow is drawing it completely out of its case, that it may be used in action. Thus ἐντείνειν stands ordinarily for דרך (as in Isa. v. 28); it also stands for משך (3 Kings xxii. 34, in A, but not in B).

The Complutensian reads ἐκτείνας ἐκτενεῖς, but to suggest that this is a likelier translation than the preceding is absurd, when we find that all the passages (about twenty in number) where ἐντείνειν is used refer to the bow, while of the numerous instances of ἐκτείνειν (ordinarily used of the stretching out of the hand) there is not one.

— ἐπὶ σκῆπτρα λέγει Κύριος. The λέγει is of course got by reading אָמַר for אֹמֶר, the Κύριος being an obvious Midrashic insertion. It is obelized in the Syro-Hexaplaric text.

The rest of the clause is not so obvious; the following seems to me at least possible. First as regards the reading: one uncial MS. (xii. of Holmes and Parsons), nine cursives, the Complutensian, and Origen (*u. s.*) read ἐπὶ τὰ σκῆπτρα. Now, may not the ἐπὶ (and especially if with the above we read ἐπὶ τὰ) be a corruption of ἑπτά, due to the translator's confusion of שְׁבֻעוֹת with שִׁבְעַת? He may originally have put ἐπὶ ἑπτὰ σκῆπτρα, and the ἐπὶ having somehow dropped, the ἑπτὰ may have been emended into ἐπὶ τὰ and so to ἐπί. Thus the verse as viewed by the original translator would refer to God's judgements done upon the "seven nations" of Canaan (Deut. vii. 1, Acts xiii. 19).

---

[1] It should be noted that the conjunction is given in the Syro-Hexaplaric.

The Septuagint Version of the Psalm. 51

One is bound to add that this corruption, if indeed it be a corruption, must be of exceeding antiquity. There is practically identity of text here in all MSS. of the LXX., except in the "four cursives," and the variation in them has no relevance here. Of the versions of the LXX., the Latin texts are unanimous in reading *sceptra*, so too the Syro-Hexaplaric. The Armenian renders the words by *upon power* or *dominion*.[1]

It remains to speak now of the text of the four cursives, Codd. 23, 62, 86, 147. The first hemistich runs in these, ὁ προεβης εξηγερθη το τοξον σου εχορτασας τας βολιδας της φαρετρας αυτου.[2] The προέβης can hardly have been anything else but a marginal variant for the ἀνέβης which these four MSS. have in the preceding clause, where the current text has ἐπιβήσῃ. The preceding word is given in Holmes and Parsons as ὁ, but it seems to me best to take it as ο', the sign for the LXX.; and to suppose that when the various reading was embodied in the text, it carried its critical mark with it.[3]

Of the following words which call for remark, ἐξηγέρθη is due to a confusion between עָרַר and עוּר; ἐχορτάσας is got from שְׁבָעוֹת misread as שָׂבַעְתָּ; βολίδας stands for מַטּוֹת, taken in the sense of "rods," the ideas of a rod, and of a spear or javelin, being sufficiently cognate. There remains φαρέτρας, which must somehow be deduced from אֹמֶר. I can propose nothing better than that there has been a confusion with אֹצָר, as suggested in Schleusner (*s. v.* φαρέτρα), the latter word meaning not only the collected treasures, but the containing receptacle[4] (see *e.g.* Jer. l. 25, "armoury" E. V.). Thus we

---

[1] I owe this statement as to the Armenian, and also the other references to the same version in this chapter, to the kindness of the Rev. Dr. S. C. Malan.

[2] Cod. 33 has αυτης, but this is, I suppose, a mere lapsus plumæ. It also omits the τάς.

[3] It is worth noting that one at least of these four cursives (Cod. 86) has itself various readings in its margin from Aquila, Symmachus, etc., so that the parent MS. would doubtless also have them.

[4] In 1 Chron. xxviii. 12, the LXX. renders it by ἀποθήκη.

should be doing no violence to language in calling a quiver a "store-house" of arrows.[1]

v. 10. λαοί. This may be due to an actual confusion between הרים and עמים, but it is perhaps more likely a change for a supposed improvement in the sense (*cf.* Exod. xix. 18). The "four cursives" have τὰ ὄρη.

— σκορπίζων ὕδατα πορείας. The first word[2] clearly presupposes זֹרֶה for זָרֵם, and πορείας may be עֲבָר, here and in Nah. i. 8. In that case, we can view the מַיִם as an instance of an absolute form, where a construct might be looked for.

As regards the structure of the Greek sentence, it would seem that we must view σκορπίζων as a nominative absolute, forming a kind of apposition to the foregoing sentence,[3] "Scattering as Thou dost the rushing waters."[4]

The comments of Augustine (*de Civ. Dei, l. c.*) and Jerome (*comm. in loc.*) show, at any rate, that they took the construction in this way, though the "hac atque hac dispergis fluenta doctrinæ" of the former, and the "Deus omnes aquas quæ a perversis dogmatibus conculcatæ sunt, disperget" of the latter are curiously different. See also "disperges" in Tert. (*adv. Marc.* iv. 39).

— ὕψος .... Here רוּם is treated as a substantive instead of doing duty as an adverb; and φαντασίας has been obtained from יָדֶיךָ, by changing ד into ר, and treating the result as some derivative of ראה. The same word occurs again in ii. 18, where it stands for מוֹרֶה, evidently read as an equivalent of מַרְאֶה.

---

[1] Their rendering of the last clause, ποταμοὺς διασκεδάσεις καὶ γῆν σείσεις, is, I suppose, simply due to treating אֶרֶץ as וְאֶרֶץ, while the two verbs are two not very exact paraphrases of תִּבְקַע, one of them perhaps due to a gloss.

[2] The Complutensian reads διασπερεῖς.

[3] Winer (*Gramm. of N. T. Greek*, § 59, 8*a*, 8*b*), speaking on the subject of apposition, refers to instances of nominatives, where a different case might have been expected. He compares Jas. iii. 8, etc., and also Mark vii. 19. In the latter case, there seems no reason why the acceptance of the reading καθαρίζων should tie us to treat the clause which it introduces as necessarily the comment of the Evangelist.

[4] *Cf.* Nahum's κατακλυσμὸς πορείας, "rushing deluge."

The Septuagint Version of the Psalm. 53

The construction of the verse will hinge upon the position of the full stop relatively to ἐπήρθη, this word being obtained by pointing נָשָׂא as though נָשָׂא. If the full stop be made to follow ἐπήρθη, in which case the punctuation will agree with that of the Hebrew, then, understanding φαντασία of the visible surface of the sea, we get the idea as seen by the Psalmist of the storm "which lifteth up the waves thereof."

Probably, however, *so far as the Greek version is concerned*, the full stop should not precede ἐπήρθη; so that the ὕψος .... is governed by ἔδωκεν. In support of this it may be noted that Cod. B puts a colon before ἐπήρθη; in Cod. A, which is distinctly stichometrical, the *stichus* runs, ἐπήρθη ὁ ἥλιος καὶ ἡ σελήνη ἔστη. Cod. א is perhaps indeterminate, though in this the line begins with ἐπήρθη. The same punctuation is also taken by the Old Latin and the Syro-Hexaplaric, and we may probably accept it therefore as representing the view of the Greek translator.

The four cursives, Codd. 23, etc., translate רָאוּךָ by ἐν τῷ ἀντοφθαλμεῖν [σε], as though they had בִּרְאוֹתְךָ. This curious word (for which see Wisd. xii. 14, Ecclus. xix. 5, Acts xxvii. 15), from the notion of looking full in the face, carries with it the notion of defiance and resistance. The phrase זֶרֶם מַיִם they paraphrase by ἐξαίσιος ὄμβρος,[1] the same adjective being also used by them for the רַבִּים of *v*. 15. Their rendering of the rest of the verse is somewhat paraphrastic; I am inclined to think that μείζων is meant to reproduce רוּם, and יָדֵיהוּ has been somehow passed over. As for ἐπέσχεν, it is clearly intransitive, "to wait" or "pause,"[2] and so, as here applied to the sun, would be equivalent to "remain high in the heavens." Perhaps therefore there has simply been a confusion between נָשָׂא and נָשָׂא.

v. 12. ὀλιγώσεις. This translation simply implies the change of the ד of תצעד into ר. The verb צָעַר only occurs in the

---

[1] Liddell and Scott (*s. v.* ἐξαίσιος) cite this very phrase from Xen. *Œc.* 5. 18.

[2] For instances of this meaning in the LXX., see Gen. viii. 10, 12; 2 Macc. v. 25.

Bible in Kal and in an intransitive sense; we may therefore assume that the translator treated the verb as though תִּצְעִיר. Curiously enough, though the verb צָעַר occurs three times in the Bible,[1] in none of these is it rendered by ὀλιγόω.[2]
The cursive MSS. 62, 86, 147, read ἐγερθήσει [Cod. 23 has ἐγέρθης, i.e. ἠγέρθης, but the Hebrew shows that this is a simple error], as though for תֵּעוֹר.

v. 12. κατάξεις. This is obviously from κατάγνυμι, not κατάγω. So it is taken by the Syro-Hexaplaric (ܬܬܒܪ); but it is curious that the Old Latin texts should be unanimous in taking it from the latter, e.g. depones (Tert.), detrahes (Jer.), dejicies (Aug.), etc. We find κατάγνυμι standing for חתת in 2 Kings (Sam.) xxii. 35, and for גדע in Jer. xlviii. 25. In the present passage, the rendering is satisfactory enough, for דוש, besides its special meaning of *threshing corn*, is used also for *crushing* generally. See e.g. Isa. xli. 15, Job xxxix. 15. Therefore there is no need to suppose that the translator assumed a reading וְתָרוּץ from the root רצץ, for that would be to assume a simultaneous action of eye-mistake and ear-mistake, which is hardly conceivable. To suppose that κατάξεις is a corruption for πατήσεις (cf. Isa. xxv. 10) is a guess as improbable as it is uncalled for.[3]

v. 13. τὸν Χριστόν σου. A considerable amount of textual authority exists for reading the plural τοὺς Χριστούς σου. It stood in Jerome's text, it is read by Cod. A and apparently by א^{cc}, by twenty-two cursives, the Complutensian and Aldine, the Syro-Hexaplaric, and by all Old Latin texts. Also the cursive MS. 23 reads τοὺς ἐκλεκτούς σου.

If we accept the view spoken of in the preceding chapter, according to which the "Anointed" means the Jewish nation, it will be seen that the difference between the singular and

---

[1] Jer. xxv. 19, Zech. xiii. 7, Job xiv. 21.

[2] We have it once, however, rendered ὀλίγοι γίγνεσθαι, Job xiv. 21; צָעִיר by ὀλιγοστός in Mich. v. 2; and מִצְעָר by ὀλίγα in Job viii. 7, 2 Chron. xxiv. 24.

[3] The four cursives, Codd. 23, etc., translate quite literally ἀλοήσεις.

plural is apparent rather than real. Though the word in Hebrew is singular, yet if the view be right which takes it collectively, the τοὺς Χριστούς σου is but of the nature of an explanation. Of the varying views adopted by the other Greek versions, it is not needful to speak again here.

v. 13. βαλεῖς. The Hebrew here is in the past tense, and so not a few MSS. of the Greek, Codd. אca, cb, one uncial (xii.) and twenty-one cursive MSS. of Holmes and Parsons, and the Aldine edition (ἔπεμψας, Complutensian). To these may be added the Syro-Hexaplaric (ܐܘܡܝܬ), and, it would seem, all forms of the Old Latin. Considering, too, that the other two finite verbs in the verse are past tenses, the βαλεῖς is at any rate open to considerable suspicion.

The clause in the Greek, "Thou wilt cast death on the heads of lawless ones," is curiously unlike the Hebrew, "Thou didst wound (dash off, shatter) the head from the house of the wicked"; yet the variations are obviously due to mere mechanical blunders. The word מָחַץ is properly to split or pierce, and is applied to the head in Judges v. 26 (רַקָּה), Psalm lxviii. 22 (רֹאשׁ). Thus βάλλειν θάνατον would be to strike death into, as though death itself were the destroying weapon. The words מבית רשע are clearly transposed, and the former word becomes מָוֶת. Thus the Hebrew is treated as involving a double accusative, "Thou didst strike into the head a deadly weapon."[1]

The cursive MSS. 23, 62, 86, 147, render the latter half of the verse, κατετόξευσας[2] κεφαλὰς ἀνθρώπων ὑπερηφάνων [this clause is omitted by Cod. 23], ἕως ἀβύσσου τῆς θαλάσσης καταδύσονται. I think we can but view this as a loose paraphrase.

— ἐξήγειρας. In עָרוֹת, the inf. Pi. of עָרָה to "lay bare," the translators have seen the root עוּר to "wake up." They may have taken it as the Kal עָרְתָ, or, as there is only one instance in the Bible of the Kal being transitive (Job xli. 2, *Krî*),

---

[1] Some writers speak of βαλεῖς .... θάνατον as being the translation of מַחֲצְתָּ, but this would be to pass over the word מבית.

[2] So מחץ is rendered in Num. xxiv. 8.

it may be safer to say Hiphil or Piel, presumably the former.[1]

v. 13. δεσμούς [יְסוֹד]. The ד being changed to a ר, we get a noun derived from the root יסר, the common word for "chastening," but also largely overlapping with the root אסר "to bind." Thus from the former root is formed the common Hiphilic noun מוֹסֵר "a bond"; see *e.g.* Ps. ii. 3, where and elsewhere the LXX. renders it by δεσμός.

— διάψαλμα. This word, the ordinary representative of *Selah* in the LXX. is omitted here by one uncial (xii. of Holmes and Parsons) and five cursive MSS. In thirteen cursives and the Aldine text, however, as well as in the text of Jerome, *Selah* is rendered by εἰς τέλος[2] (εἰς τὸ τέλος in the Complutensian); and in Cod. א^{cc}, four cursives, and the Syro-Hexaplaric the two are combined εἰς τέλος (ܠܣܘܦܐ Syro-Hexaplaric) διάψαλμα.

The rendering εἰς τέλος is that frequently adopted by the *Sexta* in the Psalms,[3] and by Theodotion in Hab. iii. 3. It is rather curious that, in the present passage, Jerome should only have been cognisant of the one reading: "ipsi LXX. rerum necessitate compulsi; qui semper *sela* interpretantur *diapsalma*, nunc transtulerunt *in finem*." This, it will be noticed, was tantamount to his own rendering *semper*.

v. 14. ἐν ἐκστάσει [בְּמָטִיר]. In what way this extraordinary translation has been arrived at must be considered very doubtful.

It may be asked first, whether there are any good grounds for doubting the correctness of the present Greek text. It has been suggested that we have here a corruption for ἐν ἐκτάσει, *i.e.* a *stretching out* of hand or staff to deliver a blow.

---

[1] The verb ἐξηγείρω occurs in the Bible in the active voice eighteen times, of which fourteen are for Hi. and four for Pi.

[2] In Smith's *Bible Dictionary* (*s. v.* Selah) the rendering εἰς τέλος is said to be that occurring in the Alexandrian MS. in Hab. iii. 13. This, however, is not so; Cod. A. reads simply διάψαλμα.

[3] See *e.g.* iii. 3, lxxvi. 4, 10 (lxxv. Gr.); *cf.* Jer. *Ep.* 29 ad *Marcellam*, § 6; Vol. I. 138.

The Septuagint Version of the Psalm. 57

This point may first be considered. Against the theory clearly may be urged the fact that no such variant is to be found in any Greek MS.[1]; that ἐν ἐκστάσει certainly underlies all forms of the Old Latin,[2] and is the original of the Syro-Hexaplaric (ܒܫܘܢܝܐ), Armenian,[3] and Arabic.

Next, it may be asked, what evidence does the LXX. itself yield as to the use of a word ἔκτασις? We find it in some MSS., including Cod. B, in Ezek. xvii. 3 for אֵבֶר, where the idea is of the long, outstretched wings of an eagle.[4] Again, in Judg. v. 22 (last clause), several MSS. and the Aldine text read τὰς ὕβρεις ἐκστάσεως αὐτῶν, the last two words standing for אַבִּירָיו.[5] One fancies that ἐκτάσεως should be read, and that there has been a blunder between אַבִּיר and אֵבֶר.

Yet once again, in Judg. xvi. 14, we read in some texts (including A and the Complutensian, but not B and the Aldine, which are altogether different) μετὰ τῆς ἐκστάσεως. Here four cursives are cited by Holmes and Parsons as reading ἐκτάσεως. There is nothing in the Hebrew for either Greek word to answer to. Montfaucon (*Hexapl., in loc.*) translates "in ecstasi," as though the reference was to the deep sleep in which Samson was; those who advocate the latter reading understanding it of the *stretched thread* of the web.[6]

To these may be added Isa. xi. 14, where Symmachus and Theodotion render מִשְׁלוֹח by ἔκτασις: "Moab shall be that on which they put forth their hands" (ἐπὶ Μωὰβ . . . . τὰς χεῖρας ἐπιβαλοῦσιν, LXX.), with which may be compared the χεὶρ ἐκτεταμένη of Jer. xxi. 4.[7]

[1] The ἐν θάμβει of the Complutensian is the only variant noted by Holmes and Parsons.

[2] Thus we have *in stupore* (Jer.), *in stupore mentis* (Aug.), *in pavore* (Mozarab. et al.), *in alienatione* (Psalt. Thomasii, etc.).

[3] Communicated by the Rev. Dr. Malan.

[4] Cod. A has ἐκστάσει, but the other reading is certainly correct.

[5] Tromm, copied by Biel and Schleusner, wrongly give אֲדִיר. There is no trace of such a reading.

[6] I do not find any evidence to justify this meaning.

[7] The reference to ἔκτασις as a translation of מטה is Judg. xv. 4, given by Schleusner (*s. v.*) is one I entirely fail to solve.

The case for ἐν ἐκτάσει is thus not a very strong one. There is a total absence of external evidence in its favour, and of the foregoing references, that in Isa. xi. 14 alone is relevant; and, besides all this, such a phrase as διακόπτειν ἐν ἐκτάσει is hardly a probable one. We must maintain then that sufficient cause has not been shown against the existing reading.

If then ἐν ἐκστάσει be accepted as the true reading, it may be well to see first in what various meanings the word is found in the LXX., etc.

It occurs then

(i) With the meaning of *fear*, whether

    (a) The feeling or state of fear, as for חֲרָדָה (Gen. xxvii. 33); פַּחַד (1 Kings [Sam.] xi. 7); מְהוּמָה (2 Chr. xv. 5); זְוָעָה (2 Chr. xxix. 8); שַׂעַר (Ezek. xxvii. 35).

    (b) The *fear-producing cause*, as for דַּבָּה (Num. xiii. 33); שַׁמָּה (Jer. v. 30).

(ii) For *trouble, flurry*, μέριμνα, as for חֲרָדָה (4 Kings iv. 13); חפז (Ps. xxx. 23).

(iii) For *stupor* or *trance*, as for תַּרְדֵּמָה (Gen. ii. 21); and, in an unnamed translation,[1] apparently for the stupor of *intoxication* in Hab. ii. 15, where the Hebrew is מִסְפֵּחַ.

(iv) For *anger*. It represents מַשְׂטֵמָה in Hos. ix. 7, in Aquila and Symmachus. [So it may be inferred from the Syro-Hexaplaric, which gives the rendering of Aquila and Symmachus for the last two words of the verse as ܣܢܐܬܐ. Jerome (*in loc.*) gives ἐγκότησις as Aquila's rendering, but perhaps there was a difference herein between the first and second edition.] Here the LXX. has μανία. It occurs also in the LXX. of Prov. xxvi. 10, due apparently to the עִבְרִים being treated as though עֶבְרָתָם.

---

[1] "Alibi translatum legi .... ἔκστασιν ὀχλουμένην, id est, amentiam turbidam."—Jerome, *in loc.*

The Septuagint Version of the Psalm. 59

The ancient versions, I believe without exception, adopt the rendering either of *stupor* or of *fear*, so that the Greek would thus be equivalent to "Thou didst pierce .... so that they are stupified with fear." Perhaps a more natural *prima facie* view of the Greek would be to make it mean "Thou didst pierce in fury . . . .," a meaning for which, as we have seen, instances can be produced from Hellenistic Greek.

It is by no means easy, however, to see how either of these could be got from the Hebrew. The suggestion that there was a confusion with some derivative of the verb תָּמַהּ would commend itself, if there were more external similarity between the words. That the confusion was with מוט is more plausible, but it lacks confirmatory evidence. Now the LXX. renders מַשְׁטֵמָה in Hos. ix. 7, 8, by μανία; and שָׂטֵי כָזָב in Ps. xl. 5 (xxxix. 5, LXX.) by μανίας ψευδεῖς; though the former means "provocation," and the latter "*apostate* liars." By no means improbably there was a confusion in both cases with the Chaldee שְׁטָא "to be mad." Conceivably the translators may have run off on this word in the passage now before us.

On the other hand, if we are to take the meaning of "fury" here, perhaps the confusion was with some derivative of שׁטם.

v. 14. σεισθήσονται. The verb σείω occurs most often by far as the rendering of רעשׁ, but stands for סַעַר in Amos i. 14; and we find συσσεισμός for סְעָרָה (or שְׂעָרָה) in 4 Kings ii. 1, Jer. xxiii. 19, Nah. i. 3. We may translate the Hebrew verb, which is in Kal in the passage before us, "sweep on like a tempest." The Kal is indeed intransitive (see Isa. liv. 11, Jon. i. 11, 13), but we had probably better assume that the translators treated the verb as a Pual (יְסֹעֲרוּ). *Cf.* Hos. xiii. 3.

— ἐν αὐτῇ. That is, ἐν τῇ ἐκστάσει. This is obtained by detaching the first two letters of the next word, and changing the לה into בה (*i.e.* בָּהּ). The διανοίξουσι represents the remainder of the word, read as יִפְצוּ. The verb פצה is translated by διανοίγειν also in Lam. ii. 16, iii. 45; and by ἀνοίγειν seven times.

v. 14. χαλινοὺς αὐτῶν. This rendering is as puzzling as any in the chapter. There appear to be no good grounds for doubting the correctness of the text. No various reading occurs (for the τὰς ἡνίας of the Complutensian cannot be considered really different), and the Syro-Hexaplaric (ܦܘܼܪ̈ܩܢܐ), Armenian,[1] and Arabic versions agree, as well as all the various forms of the Old Latin.[2] Clearly if the text is corrupt, the corruption is a decidedly ancient one.

The Hebrew word here, עֲלִיצוּת, is indeed a ἅπ. λεγ., but the verb עָלַץ occurs no less than eight times, and the cognate verb עָלַז and its derivatives are still commoner.

The most reasonable suggestion is to suppose a confusion with מְצִלּוֹת. This word, properly meaning "bells," is translated χαλινόν in Zech. xiv. 20, presumably from being supposed to refer to tinkling ornaments on the harness of the horses. Still, even if this view be taken as to the passage before us, the meaning of the Greek is far from obvious; but it is possible that χαλινοί may mean the mouth with its bit. Thus the sense will be, "They will open their bitted mouth like a beggar eating furtively and under difficulties." Here may be cited as relevant the renderings *morsus* and *ora* of the Old Latin given in the preceding note.

The order of the last three words is awkward, but it may be urged that it follows that of the Hebrew. It is true that the reading πτωχόν occurs in the Complutensian (ὡς τρώγων πτωχὸν ἐν ἀποκρύφῳ) and in one cursive; but, apart from this exceeding scantiness of evidence, it is clear that there would be every temptation to alter the nominative into an accusative, and none, so far as I can see, leading the other way. The λάθρα

---

[1] Communicated by the Rev. Dr. Malan.

[2] The renderings in Jerome and Augustine (*ll. cc.*) are *frenos* and *morsus* respectively. Thomasius's Psalter has *lora*, and the Mozarabic Breviary and some of the MSS. edited by Sabatier have *ora*. This last must be, I should suppose, a corruption of *lora*; but, at any rate, it shows the direction in which an attempt to make sense would proceed. Sabatier remarks on the rendering in Thomasius's Psalter "vocem *lora* pro *ora*," but a glance at the Greek shows that this is out of the question.

seems quite unaccountable on this latter view. The Syro-Hexaplaric may be cited, ܀ܒܪ ܡܟܣܒܬܐ ܕܩܠܒܝܗ܀, which is definite enough. Other suggestions which have been made seem strangely far fetched. For example,[1] that the translators confused the word before them with חֲלִיצוֹת (see Judg. xiv. 19, 2 Sam. ii. 21), and that they rendered it by χλαίνας, of which χαλινούς is a corruption. To this it is sufficient to say, that not only is there not the slightest trace of any such reading having ever existed, but that חֲלִיצוֹת means *exuviæ*,[2] spoils *stripped* from a conquered foe, and so can have no fitness in a passage where the sense would clearly be that of opening their own dress. Or again, to suppose that the translators, in downright helplessness, simply transliterated the Hebrew word, and that χαλινούς αὐτῶν was a bold attempt to educe sense, is surely incredible.[3]

In the four cursives, Codd. 23, 62, 86, 147, the verse runs: ἐξεδίκησας μετὰ δυνάμεως σου τοὺς ἀρχηγοὺς τῶν ἁμαρτωλῶν τοὺς πεποιθότας ἐπὶ τῇ αὐθαδείᾳ αὐτῶν ἕνεκεν τοῦ καταφαγεῖν[4] [τοὺς] πτωχοὺς λάθρα. They have of course taken נָקַבְתָּ as though נָקַמְתָּ,[5] and δύναμις represents מַטֶּה, viewed as the external symbol of power. The ἁμαρτωλῶν is less obvious; but it is not unlikely that the translator read פרזיו as פְּרִיצִים. This word is, it is true, never rendered by ἁμαρτωλός in the LXX., but Aquila, in his second edition, so rendered the word in Ezek. xviii. 10.[6] The τοὺς πεποιθότας must represent some modification of יסערו; and Schleusner suggests יסברו. Still, ע and ב are dissimilar enough; and not only do we never find סבר

---

[1] So Bos, in his *Prolegomena* to his edition of the LXX. (c. 3, *sub fin.*).

[2] In Judges (*l. c.*), the LXX. has apparently confused the word with חֲלִיפוֹת.

[3] So Lud. Cappel. (*Comm. et not. crit. in V. T.* p. 114).

[4] Cod. 23, by error, καταφυγεῖν.

[5] The verb is so rendered twenty-four times in the LXX., besides still more frequent instances of the derived substantives, which are rendered ἐκδίκησις.

[6] See Jerome (*comm. in loc.*).

rendered as above, but its meaning is rather that of looking forward, or expecting (προσδοκᾶν, ἐλπίζειν, etc., LXX.), than that of relying on, staying oneself on, as in the Greek before us. One would rather fancy the translator took the word as יִסְעָדוּ. This verb is generally transitive, but we find it intransitive in 1 Kings xiii. 7 and Prov. xx. 28; or indeed (though no case occurs in the Bible) we might point it as a passive voice. If there were sufficient authority to justify the change of שׂ and ס, one would be tempted to suppose they read יִסָּעֵנוּ, i.q. יִשָּׁעֵנוּ. This last root is several times rendered by πεποιθότες εἶναι and the like (e.g. Isa. x. 20, xxx. 12, xxxi. 1), besides four cases in which this Greek stands for שָׁעָה (as in Isa. xxxi. 1), evidently confused with שָׁעַן. The following word לְהַפְרִיאֵנִי is evidently omitted, and ἐπὶ τῇ αὐθαδείᾳ αὐτῶν is probably simply [עַל] עֲלִיצוּתָם somewhat freely interpreted, the idea being that of arrogant and wanton insolence.

v. 15. ἐπιβιβᾷς. Here the Kal of דרך has been treated as identical with the Hiphil, which occurs below, *v.* 19.

— ταράσσοντας. It is clear that the translators have misread חֹמֶר as though חֹמְרִים. The verb חמר has been rendered by ταράσσειν in Ps. xlvi. 4 (xlv. 4 Gk.); and, one might even add in *v.* 3, for, coming in such close proximity, the rendering of הָמִיר by ταράσσεσθαι is quite suggestive of a blunder between ה and ח. See also Lam. i. 20, ii. 11.

v. 16. ἐφυλαξάμην. This careless confusion between שמע and שמר occurs also 3 Kings xi. 38, Prov. xix. 37.

— κοιλία. The reading καρδία is supported by the Aldine text, seventeen of Holmes and Parsons' cursives, and the Syro-Hexaplaric (ܒܠܒ), and it may be noted that בֶּטֶן is rendered by καρδία in Prov. xxii. 18. Still בֶּטֶן is so common a word, and κοιλία is its so constant translation, that there is no reason for disturbing the common text.

— προσευχῆς. Here a noun comes in where in the Hebrew is the verb צָלַלְוּ. The origin of the blunder is obvious, though the resulting Greek text does not give much sense. The trans-

The Septuagint Version of the Psalm. 63

lator dropped one ל, and then read צלי, from the Chaldee root צלא "to pray" (see *e.g. Targ. Onk.* Gen. xviii. 22, Ex. xvii. 12).

v. 16. ὑποκάτωθεν. The Hebrew תַּחְתָּי in this passage is simply "where I stand," "in loco meo." The LXX., though somewhat too literal, clearly understood this sense.

— ἡ ἕξις μου. This is somehow got from אֲשֶׁר, but it is absurd to suggest, as has been done, that it was a confusion with אֹשֶׁר, because *happiness* is the basis of physical well-being! Possibly there might have been a confusion with אֲשׁוּרִי or אַשּׁוּרִי, that is, a course of going, and so one's state. More likely, however, is it that something connected with יֵשׁ was thought of. Twice in the Bible (2 Sam. xiv. 19, Mic. vi. 10) this appears in a semi-Aramæanized form, אָשׁ, which brings us nearer.[1]

There does not seem to be much ground for doubting the correctness of the text, though ἰσχύς is found in some authorities. The last-named reading is found in six (or perhaps rather five) cursives and in the Complutensian; it was also that found in Jerome's text.[2] On the other hand, the great mass of MSS. read ἕξις,[3] which was also the reading of Augustine (*habitudo*) as well as that in other Old Latin texts[4]; and this further has the support of the Syro-Hexaplaric (ܡܩܘܡܐ).[5]

In Lam. iv. 7, Symmachus renders אָדְמוּ עֶצֶם by πυρρότεροι τὴν ἕξιν, where the Syro-Hexaplaric has the same word as in our present passage.

The four cursive MSS. (23, 62, 86, 147) have, as usual, a totally different translation. The following points may be

---

[1] In face of the other reading ἰσχύς, it may be worth remarking that the noun from the same root, תּוּשִׁיָּה, is translated ἰσχύς in Job xii. 16.

[2] *Fortitudo mea, sive ut alibi scriptum reperimus, ἡ ἕξις μου, quod nos possumus dicere, habitudo mea; diversa quippe exemplaria reperiuntur.* (*Comm. in loc.*).

[3] One cursive reads ὑπόστασις.

[4] The text in the Mozarabic Breviary reads *virtus*, which occurs also in Thomasius's Psalter and some other texts.

[5] In the margin of the Ambrosian MS. εξισμου is written.

64   *The Septuagint Version of the Psalm.*

noted. We find ἐταξάμην in the place of ἐφυλαξάμην, the Hebrew being presumably read as שַׂמְתִּי,[1] though it is perhaps possible that it, like the ordinary reading, is to be referred to שמר. The צללו now disappears altogether. We have רקב rendered by τρόμος, which, the character of the version in these four MSS. being considered, is probably a sort of Midrash; and we need not suppose a confusion with רָעַד, for which or רְעָדָה, τρόμος stands six times in the LXX.

The latter part of the verse (from the Ethnakh onwards) in these four MSS. runs, ταῦτα φυλάξῃς εἰς ἡμέραν (or ἐν ἡμέρᾳ) θλίψεως ἐπαγαγεῖν ἐπὶ ἔθνος[2] πολεμοῦν τὸν λαόν σου. How the first two words can be got from the Hebrew I quite fail to see. The ἐπαγαγεῖν is clearly used in a seemingly intransitive sense " to march against a nation that wars with[3] Thy people." This, viewed as a paraphrase, can be got from the Hebrew.

v. 16. παροικίας. " The people of my sojourning," *i.e.* " those among whom I am a sojourner." The LXX. of course saw here in the Hebrew יגודנו, not the root גוד, but גור; and perhaps doubling the final *mem* of עם, they made the next word into מְגוּרַי.

v. 17. βρώσεως. The foregoing βρῶσιν shows that instead of taking מכלה, as it really is, from the root כלא, the translator foolishly referred it to אכל, as though it were מַאֲכָלָה and a feminine equivalent of מַאֲכָל.

After φάτναις, Cod. A and one of Holmes and Parsons' uncials (Cod. xii.) and two cursives add ἐξιλάσεως αὐτῶν. This word only occurs elsewhere in the LXX. in Num. xxix. 11, for כִּפֻּרִים. Clearly, however, ἐξιλάσεως is a corruption for ἐξ

---

[1] τάσσω stands for שׂים in the LXX. nearly forty times, including one passage in the present chapter (*v.* 19), though there the four cursives have κατέστησε.

[2] In Cod. 23, for ἐπὶ ἔθνος ...., stands εφενος πολεμου, the other three reading as above. The Hebrew makes it plain that the latter reading must be a mere corruption of the preceding.

[3] The construction πολεμεῖν τινα is very common in the LXX. See *e.g.* Num. xxi. 26, Josh. ix. 2, and often.

The Septuagint Version of the Psalm. 65

ἰάσεως, which is actually the reading of one cursive. This has been a second rendering of בִּרְפָתִים, treated as בִּרְפָאוּתָם. See Prov. iii. 8.

v. 19. εἰς συντελείαν [כָּאַיָּלוֹת]. The reading ὡς ἐλάφων is found in three cursives, and ὡς ἐλάφου in three cursives, and in Theodoret (*In Cant. Cant.* c. 2; Vol. II. 64). It is, however, simply a conforming to the Hebrew. The word συντέλεια is of frequent occurrence in the LXX., and ordinarily for some derivative of the root כלה; perhaps תַּכְלִית (Job xxvi. 10) would be the nearest. The meaning is doubtless, "He will set my feet in a state of perfect safety," though "utter destruction" is the most ordinary meaning in the LXX.

The four cursives (Codd. 23, etc.) render the word by ἀσφαλεῖς, either from the same general idea as that of the current text, or by some confusion with אַיֶּלֶת.

— τὰ ὑψηλά. This, save for the omission of the promominal affix, is a literal translation of the Hebrew. The four cursives, Codd. 23, etc., have the curious Midrash καὶ ἐπὶ τραχήλους τῶν ἐχθρῶν μου. This same translation also occurs in Deut. xxxiii. 29.

— τοῦ νικῆσαι [לַמְנַצֵּחַ]. "That I should prevail." Considering the great frequency of the Hebrew word in the headings of the Psalms, it is a little singular that we should have here a different translation. Whatever root-meanings the verb נצח may include, the meaning of power or innate strength is clearly to be taken; see *e.g.* 1 Chron. xxix. 11, where we have νίκη for נֵצַח. In the four cursives, Codd. 23, etc., after ἐπιβιβᾷ με, stand the words ταχίσας (καθήσας, Cod. 23) κατεπαύσατο. I am strongly inclined to doubt whether these words are to be taken as representing the Hebrew, however disguised. Some have suggested that some form from נוח was taken for מְנַצֵּחַ, but this does not take us very far; and I prefer to consider the words to have originated as a remark appended by some scribe; the subject of the verb being the Prophet, who, his task finished, ceases. This is made more probable by the clause not being prefaced by any connecting particle.

www.ingramcontent.com/pod-product-compliance
Lightning Source LLC
Chambersburg PA
CBHW020253090426
42735CB00010B/1905